Y0-CKP-997

ROBERT LOUIS STEVENSON
ELEMENTARY LIBRARY
FRIDLEY, MINNESOTA 55421

THE WHOLE MIRTH CATALOG

THE Whole Mirth Catalog

A SUPER Complete Collection of Things

MICHAEL SCHEIER & JULIE FRANKEL

Franklin Watts
New York | London | 1978

Any resemblance to real people, places, products, or situations is purely coincidental.

Copyright © 1978 by Michael Scheier and Julie Frankel
All rights reserved.
Printed in the United States of America
5 4 3 2 1

Library of Congress Cataloging in Publication Data

Scheier, Michael.
 The whole mirth catalog.

 SUMMARY: A collection of jokes, cartoons, puns, and humorous games, crafts, and projects.
 1. American wit and humor. 2. Wit and humor, Juvenile. [1. Wit and humor. 2. Jokes] I. Frankel, Julie, joint author. II. Title.
PN6163.S34   817'.5'408   78-6473
ISBN 0-531-02494-6
ISBN 0-531-02226-9 lib. bdg.

TABLE of CONTENTS

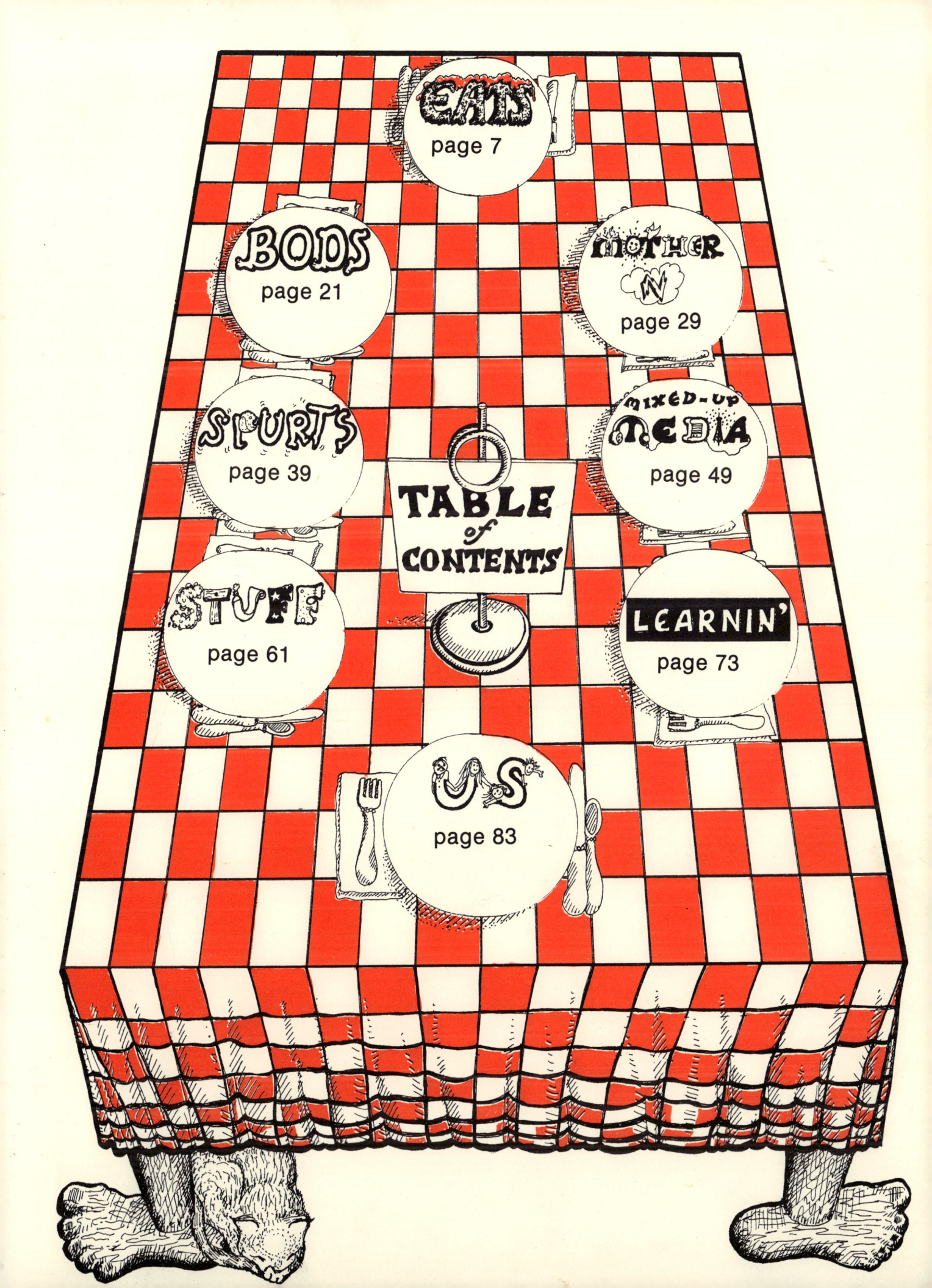

- EATS — page 7
- BODS — page 21
- MOTHER N — page 29
- SPURTS — page 39
- MIXED-UP MEDIA — page 49
- STUFF — page 61
- LEARNIN' — page 73
- US — page 83

"Flip my corners!"

page 6

page 7

EATS

A Mirth Close-up

How food is delivered throughout your body

page 8

Charmees

Ingredients: plastic, vinyl, rubber, chrome, paper, cellophane, polyester, preservatives, flour, and sugar.

Nutritional Information: 0% of the Minimum Daily Requirement.

EXCITING RECIPE

Make MULIES with CHARMEES—
1. Blend one box CHARMEES with 2 bags MARZMELLOWS. (No need to even open the CHARMEES box; the cardboard adds unique flavor!)
2. Refrigerate MULIES until rock hard.
3. Test for doneness. Drop MULIES on floor. If floor cracks then MULIES are done.

PLUS ⬇

LIMITED TIME ONLY
1 Edible Plate
inside *every* box!
Get the whole set!

Charmees

HELPS BODIES GROW (maybe)

13 FLAVORS collect 'em ALL!

Our Guarantee: every box has ONE free piece of cereal.

For those meals that are sooooooooooooo scrumptious you can't bear to miss a drop, try eating on EDIBLE PLATES! Eat the delicious meal; then eat the plate!

FOOD CHECKERS

Gather the pieces . . .

Use 12 chocolate chip cookies and 12 creme-filled cookies,

or

for more nutritious FOOD CHECKERS . . .

Use 12 carrot slices and 12 cucumber slices

Use your regular checkerboard,

or

draw one yourself on heavy paper or cardboard.

Play checkers! Eat the pieces as you jump them! Keep a few extra cookies on the side for kings.

It's not FAIR when...

. . . egg yolks break!

. . . icing sticks to the wrapper!

page 10

We think FOOD FUN FAIR is the restaurant of the future. We present their menu as a public service!!

RATING: 5 greasy spoons

FOOD FUN FAIR

Eat what you want — the way you want!

FOODFIGHT ROOM

PLEASE PLAY WITH YOUR FOOD

If it can be eaten, it can be thrown. Come in and play awhile. Parents not admitted!

ALL YOU CAN THROW $1.25

FOOD-ART ROOM

SANDCASTLE MASHED POTATOES
Special recipe lets you mold hills, valleys, moats, bridges, tunnels, anything! $1.10

GALLON-O'-GRAVY
For rivers, oceans, and just making designs! .... 35¢

SQUISHY WHITE BREAD
Served warm and fresh.

Stick your whole arm into a loaf and mold fistfuls of bread into balls!
Three loaves .... 75¢

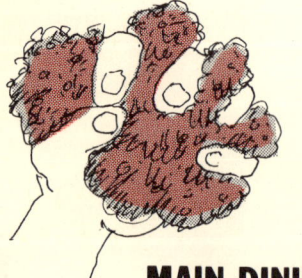

CHOPPED MEAT CLAY
Comes in a large bowl. Squeeze until it oozes through your fingers. Sculptor on duty to help with portraits $1.85

MAIN DINING ROOM

QUARTER-POUND CREME-FILLED COOKIE
You've never had anything like it! .... 60¢

ICE CREAM SOUP
Served in hard balls. You stir it, and stir it, and stir it until it's soup.   Cup .... 25¢   Bowl .... 45¢

BANANA MUSH
Whole bananas served right into
your hands. Squeeze them! Mush them!
Then peel back the skin and
watch the banana MUSH drip out! .... 15¢

SPAGHETTI SLURPER
Ingenious machine feeds you one
super-long strand at a time! $1.25

MULTI-STRAW
(with drink of your choice)
Blows weird bubbles and amplifies
the strange sounds .... 35¢

EGG YOLKS ONLY .... 25¢

BOWL-O'-BATTER
Supply your own finger .... 40¢

FOOD FREAK SPECIAL
Six-legged chicken for six $4.25

FANTASTIC FLIPS
Served at your table. Use your hands
or our own super-springy flippers.
Flip 'em yourself: PANCAKES .... 95¢
　　　　　　　　　　PIZZA $2.50

COLD CATS—a mystery food .... 45¢

SIDE ORDERS

WHIPPED CREAM　　in bowl ... 65¢; in sprayer ... 30¢

TUB-O'-SYRUP
to drown pancakes .... 15¢

CUSTARD THROW-PIES .... 50¢ each

If you do not wish to eat with your hands, please notify us in advance. An extra charge of $5 will be made for knives, forks and spoons!

SPECIAL COMBO ORDERS AVAILABLE!

If you don't see it .... ask for it!

page 12

Why pack a messy candy bar when you can SPRAY SPARERIBS?

SPRAY SPARERIBS are fun!
SPRAY them on your plate!
SPRAY them in your hand!
SPRAY them anywhere!
Any time! Any place!
And just try to say
SPRAY SPARERIBS ten times fast!

I like SPRAY SPARERIBS because they're so easy and convenient to give Billy for lunch!

RECORD! RECORD! RECORD! RECORD! RECORD

From the INNER PEAS FOUNDATION

Includes 2 Big Hits:
ROCK-A-BYE BROCCOLI
&
CHICKEN LULLABY

Also available in cassettes!

Play the record for your food while making a meal!

ROCK-A-BYE BROCCOLI READY FOR FUN!... WHEN THE WATER BOILS, YOU'RE ABOUT... WHEN THE STEAM BLOWS, THE TOP WILL COME OUT AND DONE WILL START TO ROCK...

BROCCOLI
INNER PEAS FOUNDATION

Your food will be happier!

Write for free catalog.
Send $10 to cover mailing costs!

ROCKET STRAWS has finally done it!
Anyone can blow the paper off a straw,
but now you can AIM, GUIDE, and even DIRECT it!
95% accurate aim! TWICE as fast as regular straws!

VEGETABLE DIGEST presents:

Pimple Food by Ed Ibble

New exciting recipes! Sure to be a best seller! If you don't want to use the recipes in the book, then use the book in your recipes! Pages are made from pressed apricots. They're DELISH!

Chocolate Malted Milk Shake: To one glass of milk, add 1 tablespoon chocolate malt powder and 1 scoop ice cream. Stir. Drink mixture. Jump up and down until your shake is shaken.

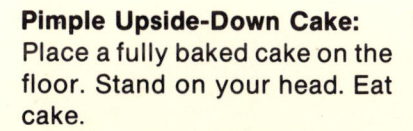

Pimple Upside-Down Cake: Place a fully baked cake on the floor. Stand on your head. Eat cake.

Mom and Pop Popped Toe Corns: Ask parents and grandparents to save their toe corns. When you have enough, put them in the popper and roast them. Serve with melted butter and salt to taste.

Filet of Sole: Take six soles and place in pan. Dot with butter. Season to taste. Broil 10 minutes on each side. Serve piping hot.

Eggbeater arrested for cruelty!

THE Dip 'N Dip KIDS

Panel 1: "Gee, it's sure HOT today!" "YEAH! Let's go swimming in Sue's pool." "NAH! She never has any food. Let's go over to Joan's for some FOOD!"

Panel 2: "Let's do BOTH!" "HOW?!?"

Panel 3: "Come on over to my house — You'll see..." "???"

Panel 4: "...with THIS!"

Panel 5: DIP 'N DIP

Panel 6: "See, I just pour DIP 'N DIP in my pool. In 5 minutes the water starts to get thick and creamy"

Panel 7: "Yeah! And it tastes great, too!" "WOW! This is terrific — you can really float in it!"

Panel 8: "Yup! With DIP 'N DIP you can swim as much as you want — eat as much as you want ... and never leave the pool!"

SPECIAL OFFER!
Buy 10 boxes of DIP 'N DIP, send proof of purchase plus $2 and get 1 dozen
DIP 'N CHIP EAT-RAFTS
made of 100% DEE-LISH-US potato chips!

page 15

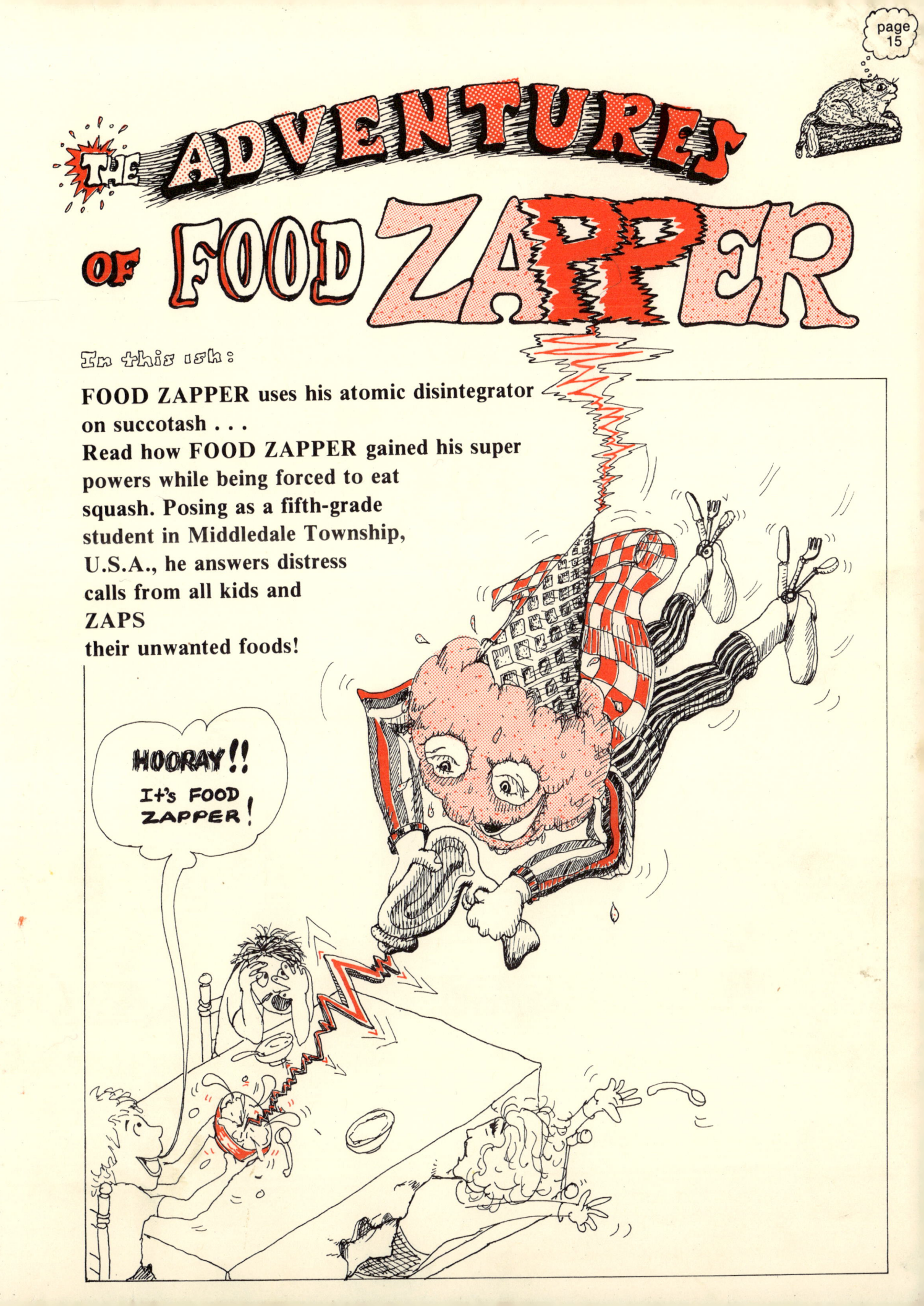

THE ADVENTURES OF FOOD ZAPPER

In this ish:

FOOD ZAPPER uses his atomic disintegrator on succotash...
Read how **FOOD ZAPPER** gained his super powers while being forced to eat squash. Posing as a fifth-grade student in Middledale Township, U.S.A., he answers distress calls from all kids and **ZAPS** their unwanted foods!

HOORAY!! It's FOOD ZAPPER!

page 16

SMELLY JEWELRY PROJECT
SARDINE NECKLACE

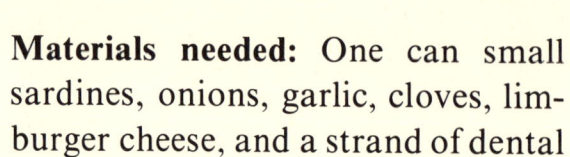

Materials needed: One can small sardines, onions, garlic, cloves, limburger cheese, and a strand of dental floss.

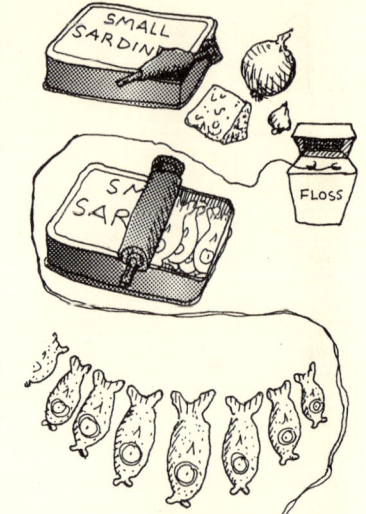

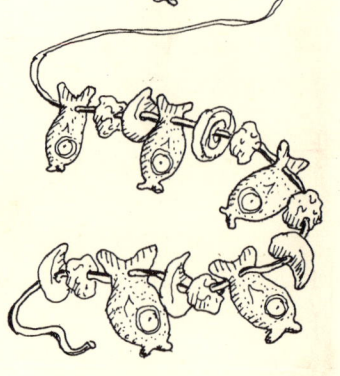

Handy instructions:
1. Open tin of sardines (carefully).
2. Remove each fish and arrange according to size. Put the largest fish in the center.
3. Tear off a strand of dental floss.
4. String each fish onto the floss, alternating with a piece of garlic, onion, or cheese.
5. Tie both ends of the necklace together.
6. Wear on a warm day. *Your friends will recognize you even before they see you!*

NEW GAME: ICE CREAM HOT POTATO

1. On a HOT day get together with a group of friends.
2. Form a circle.
3. Pass a scoop of hard ice cream from one person to the next until there is no more!

page 17

You know how sometimes those cravings come on you???
And you can never have exactly what you want to eat???
GOBBLE PRODUCTS has the answer!! Arm yourself against
the attack of the crawling munchies and get

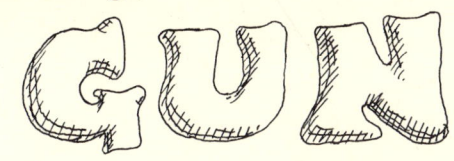

GOBBLE GUN

GOBBLE GUN has it all. Strap it to your waist whenever you go out. Just dial the food you want to GOBBLE. Special micro-packaging makes it possible to include 872 food varieties: chocolate, soda pop, pizza, ice cream, cereal, milk, cookies, hamburger, hot dog, and MORE! MORE! MORE! MORE! MORE! MORE! MORE!

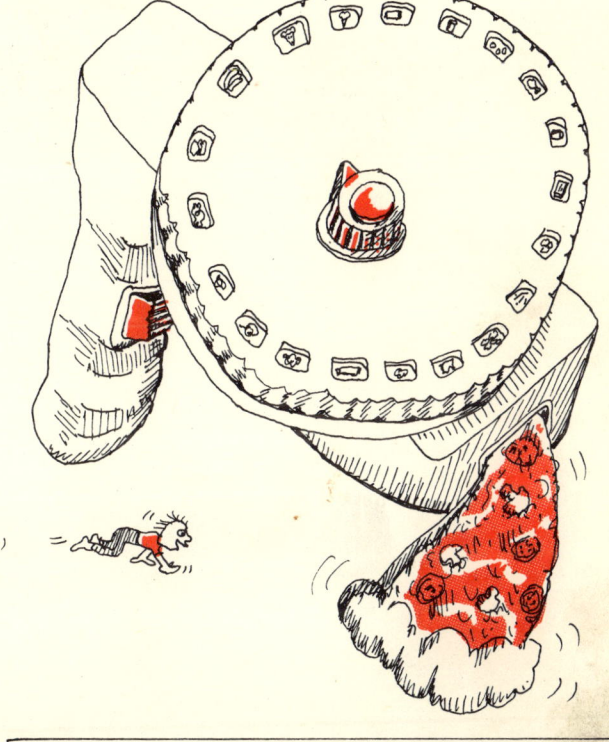

THE NEWEST HELPING HAND

Now at last you can eat with your hand, your HELPING HAND! The NEWEST UTENSIL!

So MANY USES!
A spoon,
a backscratcher,
a page turner,
a nose picker,
a telephone cradle,
a hand-me-down.

Anything you can do with your hand, you can do with HELPING HAND!!!

MOVIE POSTER

FRANKEN FÜRTER MEETS THE BEANS FROM OUTER SPACE

page 18

INTERNATIONAL SALAD DRESSINGS

FRENCH Lettuce/Cabbage PULLOVER

ITALIAN Tomato PAJAMAS

RUSSIAN Onion WARMER

BLUE CHEESE Celery DUNGAREES

for those people who don't like naked salads. Surveys have shown that 3 out of 4 salads would rather be dressed than undressed.

Bunch of Bananas

Tuna Fish

page 19

Strawberry Traffic Jam

Just One Soup

Sloppy Joe's

Egg Salad

Black Eyed Peas

Club Sandwich Clubhouse

page 20

Try this for real!

CUP CUP CAKE

Major ingredients: **CUP CAKES**

Buy them in the market or bakery ← EASIEST AND MOST EXPENSIVE
Make them from a mix
Make them from scratch ← HARDEST AND CHEAPEST

SAUCERS

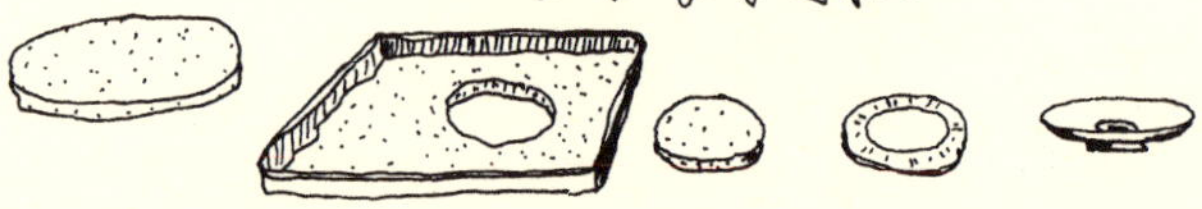

Use flat, round, toastable muffins; round, flat cakes cut from a sheet cake; a small paper plate covered with icing, or a regular china saucer.

Trim off top of cupcake so it is flat. Scoop out a shallow circle on top. Ice cupcake and saucer separately. Put cupcake on top of saucer. Fill scooped-out circle on top with melted chocolate or powdered cocoa mix. Top with a glop of icing or whipped cream. (Candle is optional.) Attach handle.

HANDLE MATERIAL

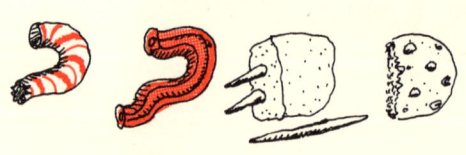

Use a cut-down candy cane,
licorice,
a piece of cake
or cookie cut in a small semicircle.

Decorate cup cupcake any way that appeals to you. Make a design with sprinkles, nuts, raisins, or seeds. Add tiny flower designs or run a stripe around the edge of the cup and the saucer.

ICING

Buy it in a can premade or make it from a recipe.

BODS

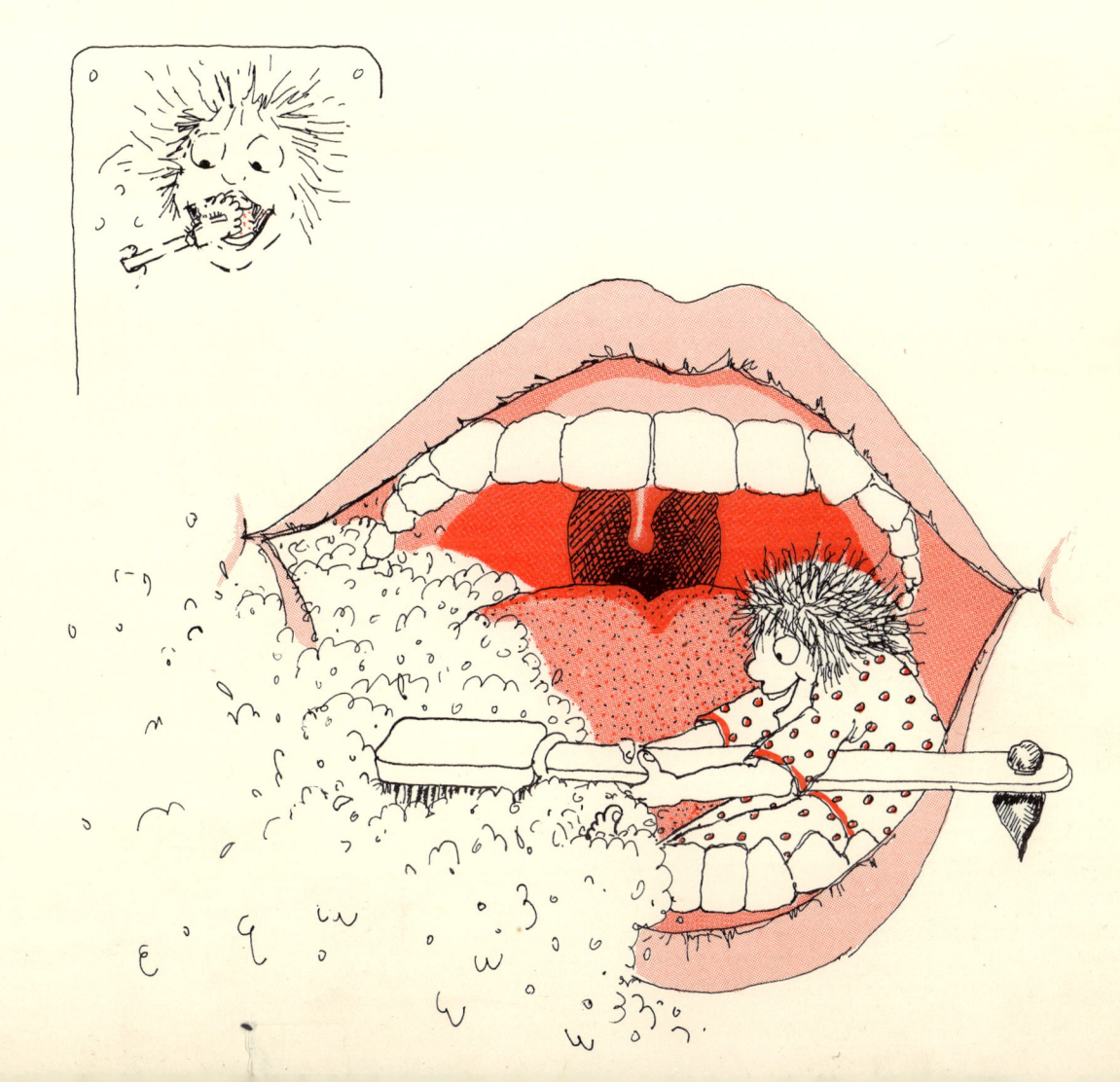

page 22

DOCTOR TUMMY'S AMAZING Behind-the-Scenes Never-Before-Revealed BODY MAP of Things That Ail You

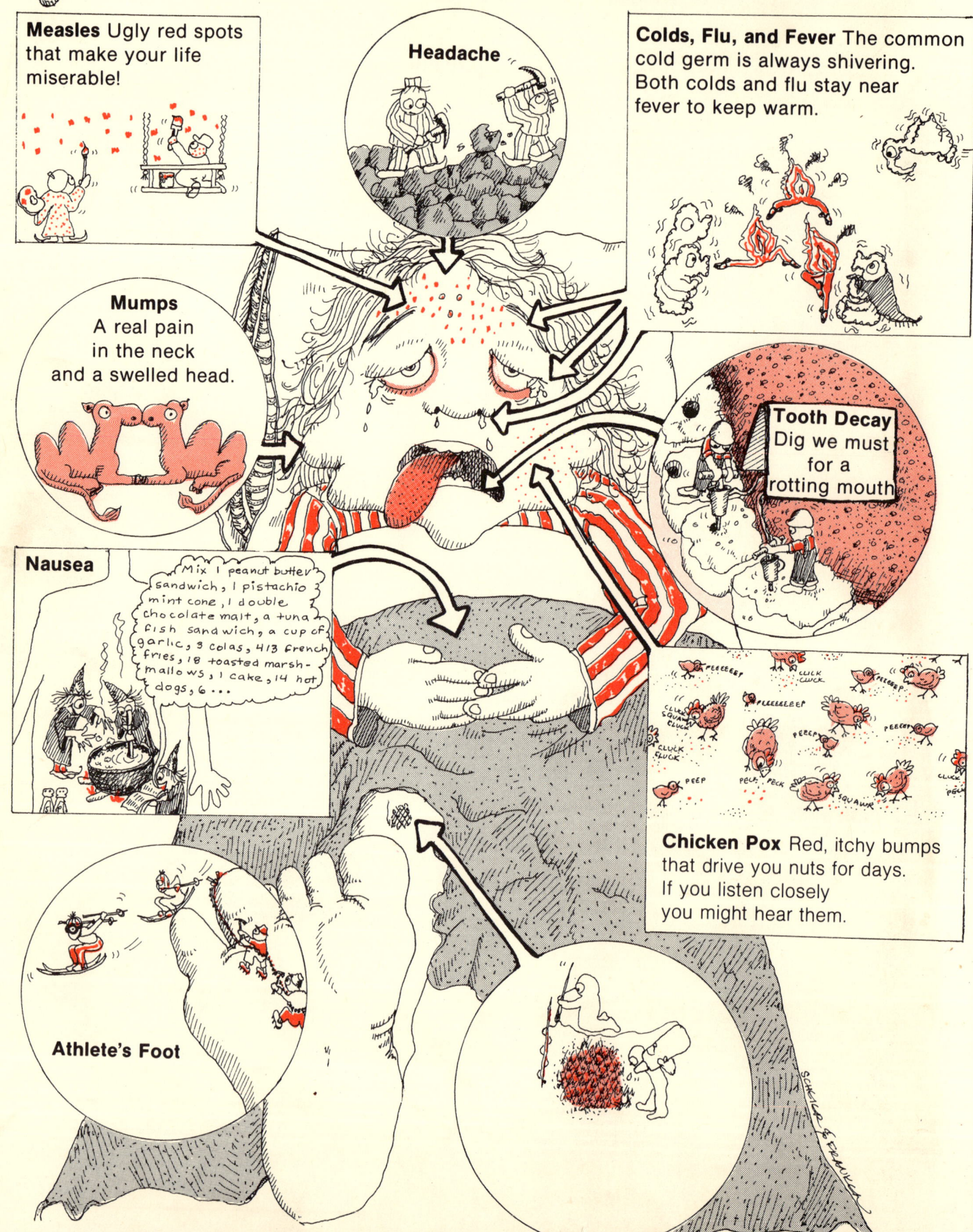

Measles Ugly red spots that make your life miserable!

Headache

Colds, Flu, and Fever The common cold germ is always shivering. Both colds and flu stay near fever to keep warm.

Mumps A real pain in the neck and a swelled head.

Tooth Decay Dig we must for a rotting mouth

Nausea

Mix 1 peanut butter sandwich, 1 pistachio mint cone, 1 double chocolate malt, a tuna fish sandwich, a cup of garlic, 3 colas, 413 french fries, 18 toasted marshmallows, 1 cake, 14 hot dogs, 6 . . .

Chicken Pox Red, itchy bumps that drive you nuts for days. If you listen closely you might hear them.

Athlete's Foot

HOW TO GET RID OF HICCUPS

Sneak up on yourself and scream.

Pretend you have to bring them to school for homework; lose them.

Hold your breath while blowing up a balloon and whistling "Rudolph the Red-Nosed Reindeer!"

Make a deal—if the hiccups don't bother you, you won't bother them!

Count them!

Trap them in a jar. Refuse to let them out until they go away.

Record them on a tape deck and play them back while hiccuping.

Burp!

Time the spaces between hiccups. Pretend you have to graph it for math homework.

Go to the nearest haunted house.

Learn to live with them; they're pretty cute.

If people think they get warts from touching toads ...

what do toads think they get from being touched by people?

LOOK OUT! You'll get smooth!

A MIRTH MOVIE SPECIAL

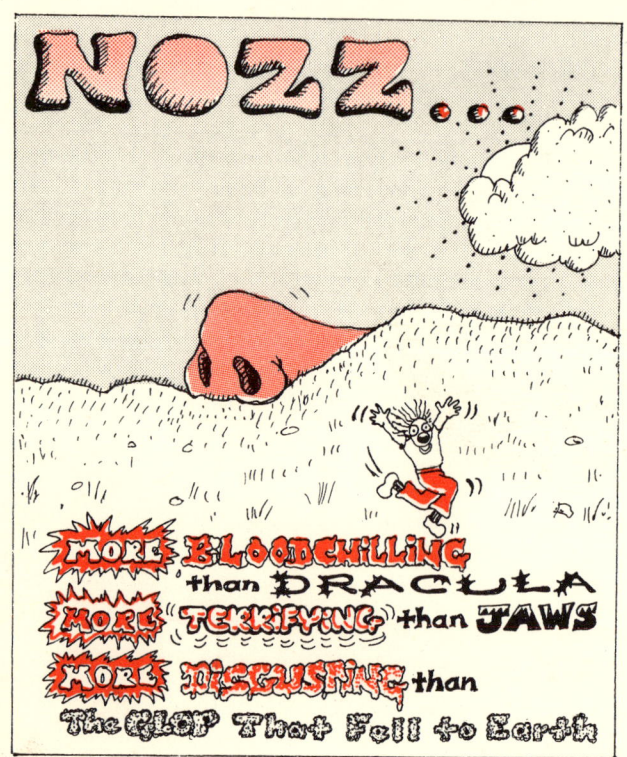

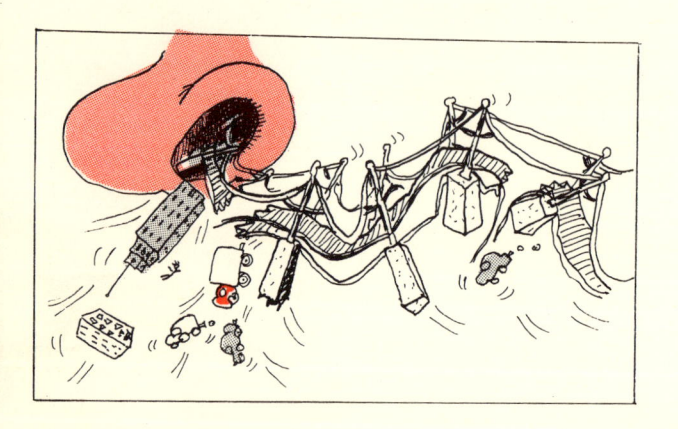

NOZZ...

More BLOODCHILLING than DRACULA
More TERRIFYING than JAWS
More DISGUSTING than The BLOB That Fell to Earth

NOZZ is not recommended for the weak-kneed. This film is often eerie, but mostly it's nosey. It will make your nose run cold.

NOZZ opens at the North Pole in a scientific research station. An experimental atomic shovel blows up, killing everyone. The explosion unearths and gives new life to the creature NOZZ, buried alive for centuries.

NOZZ was the last survivor of a race of nose beings that came from another planet 100 million years ago. NOZZ roams the earth burying cities anytime it sneezes. In one action scene it sucks up all of Tokyo when it inhales. Armies try flame-throwers, atomic weapons, but NOZZ only gets fiercer. Finally a young country doctor fearlessly examines NOZZ and concludes that the monster has a cold. A team of scientists make penicillin harpoons, a brigade of mothers load dump trucks with homemade chicken soup, and a local bug spray company works around the clock to make the world's largest atomizer filled with nasal mist.

NOZZ is treated, cured, and becomes a friend to the world by putting out forest fires with a single sneeze, breathing in air pollution wherever it occurs, and tracking missing persons around the world.

One final caution: Do *not* see NOZZ if you suffer from asthma!

HOLD THE HOSES, IT'S NOZZ!!

How to solve pimple problems??

Put a bag over your head!!

page 25

NO MORE UNWANTED BATHS!!!

RING-AROUND-THE-BATHTUB

RING-AROUND-THE-BATHTUB... and away goes bathing down the drain

Directions: Go into bathroom; close door. Fill tub. Sprinkle in RING-AROUND-THE-BATHTUB: stir it around. Make bathing sounds.
DO NOT GET IN TUB!
Let water out. In a few short minutes your tub will be coated with a film of grime that will make it look as if you had taken the bath of your life.
98% effective;
guaranteed to convince ANY parent.

If people were meant to bathe they would have been born in a bathtub!!

page 26

Mirth
FEATURED COMPANY OF THE YEAR

You mean practical jokes?

For excellence in the field of practical products made with humor

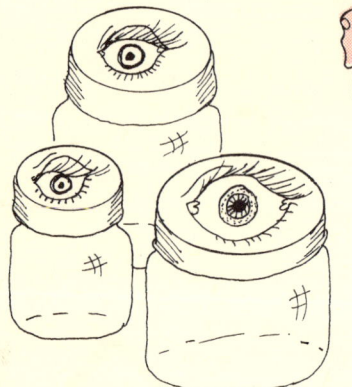

PART-ICLES, Inc.
Your parents will frazzle!
Your friends will howl!

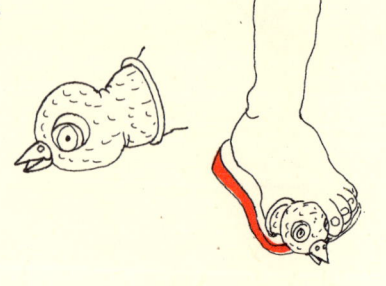

Eyeball these EYE-lids.

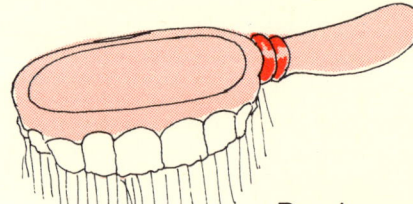

Brush away dandruff with this TOOTH-brush.

Click your heels in a pair of PIGEON-toes.

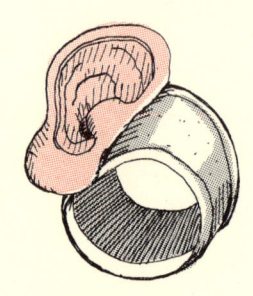

Listen to your EAR-ring.

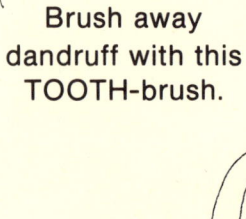

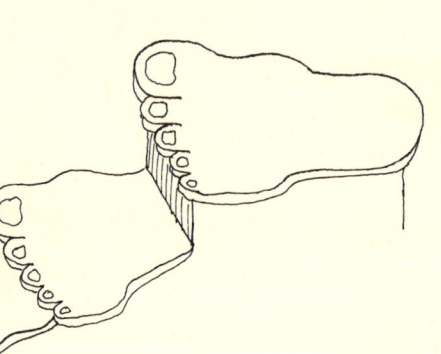

Stand on your own FOOT-steps.

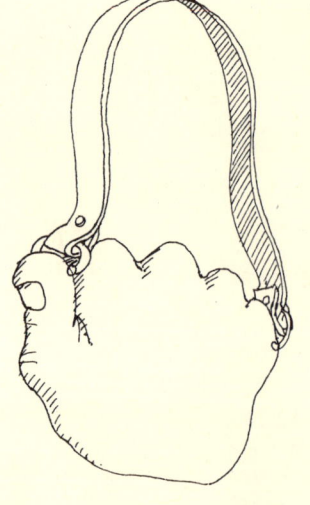

Handle this HAND-bag.

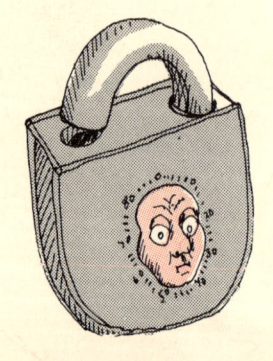

Lock your locker in a combination-HEAD-lock.

Put your foot in your mouth or suck your thumb with all-day FOOT-and-THUMB suckers.

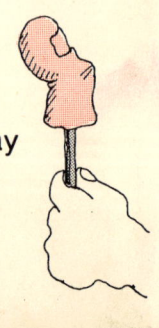

HOW TO STAY IN BED 10 EXTRA MINUTES!

page 27

Pretend you're asleep.

Make believe you're a bump on a log.

Cross off extra days on the calendar and say it's Saturday.

Paste black paper on the windows and say it's the middle of the night.

Sleep under your bed.

Put the dog in *your* bed; you sleep in the dog house.

Say you're sleeping for all the people in the world who can't sleep.

Build a stone wall outside your room.

Put these signs on your door:

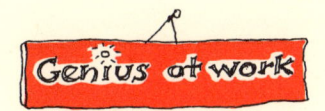

WILL RETURN IN 0 MINUTES

OUT TO LUNCH

Genius at work

DO NOT DISTURB

OH PLEASE
OH PLEASE
OH PLEASE
OH PLEASE
OH PLEASE
PLEASE
PLEASE
PLEASE
PRETTY
PLEASE
PLEASE
PLEASE

When all else fails . . . BEG!!!

Hey! Eight eyes!!

FANCASTIC!!

Try this for real!

**FANCASTIC!
You've broken your arm, your leg, your whatever!
Now you can decorate it!**

Get friends to sign it.

Draw a picture of *your* broken bone on it.

Put road signs on it.

Get someone with lipstick to plant a kiss on it.

Add decals, labels, stamps, and stickers.

Tie it with ribbon, streamers, and doodads.

Go wild with graffiti art.

Add riddles, jokes, and even puzzles and mazes.

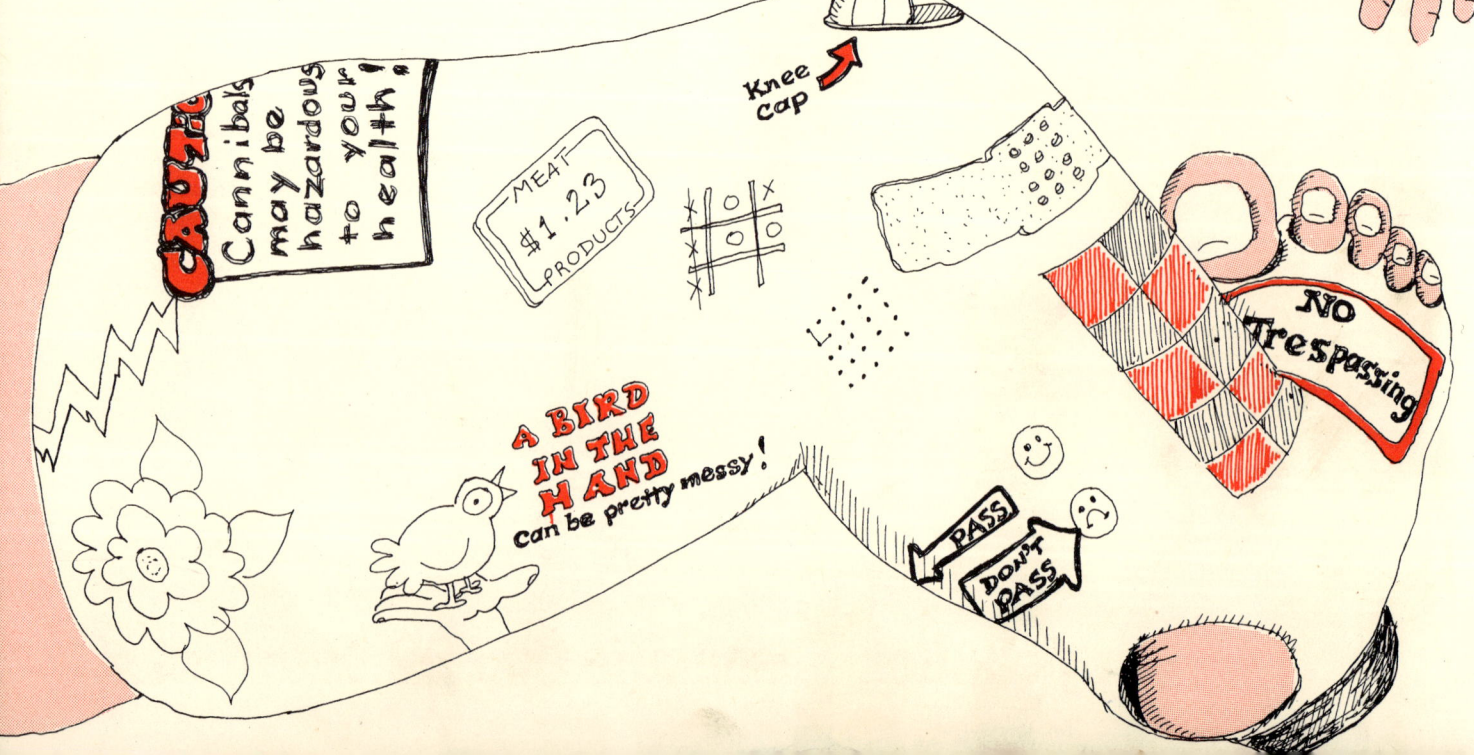

MOTHER

page 29

A Mirth Close-up
Air pollution—magnified 5,000,000 times

page 30

Nature Identification of Animals We Rarely See

How do you recognize the 50-foot (15.2-m), ten-toed, spiny-tailed, scaly-stomached **Decatarantulant?**

Lucky for us!

Answer: You can't miss it! Just hope it misses you!

FOOD CHAIN bracelet

hand crafted in genuine Sterling Liver

Bird Burgers

Collect some old onion bags or any plastic mesh.

Save as much raw fat as you can, or ask the butcher for some. (Raw fat is called suet.)

Mush the fat together and stuff it into the onion bag, or wrap the mesh around it.

Stick a couple of sticks all the way through the stuffed bag and out the other side. Make the sticks cross. This makes a nice perch for the birds.

Tie the bag up really tight, winding the string around, but don't totally cover the fat. You have just made a BIRD BURGER. Hang it outside near a window, or from a tree.

If you live in the city, go to a nearby park and hang it from a tree. Go a short distance away and be patient. It takes the birds awhile to find it. Works best in cooler weather.

ORGANIC Bird Burgers

Get a pine cone.
Smear it with peanut butter or fat.
Sprinkle or roll it in seeds.
Tie a string to it firmly.
Hang it!

Try this for real!

Birds are attracted to bright colors.

Tie red ribbons or red tape to your burgers!

page 32

OUT TO PICNIC

Do woodpeckers get headaches?

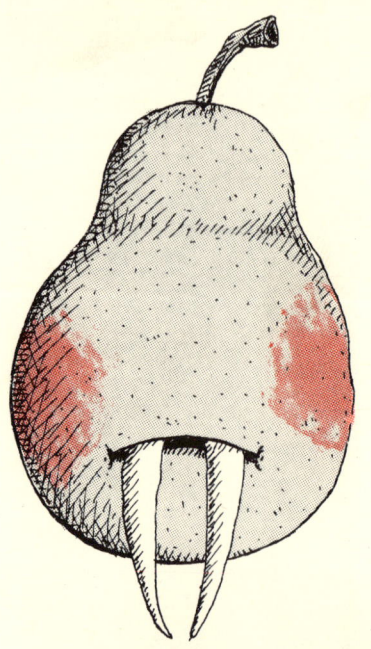

A VAMPEAR

1001 KIDS

Do fish smell?

Waiter! Waiter! There's a man in my soup!

page 33

Dog's best friend

If anteaters eat ants, then . . . what's an anteater-eater?

Can lovebirds get divorced?

Can you find the zookeeper?

Can you find the person who fed the bear?

What's red and green and gives to the poor?

ROBINHOOD ROBIN

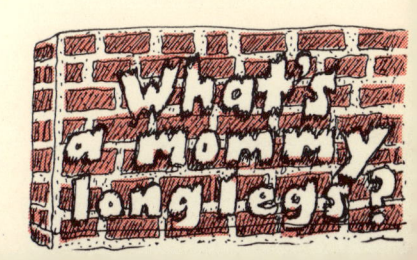

What's a mommy long-legs?

page 34

Do you sometimes wish you could sprout wings??????????

Now it is finally possible

with WINGBAT'S

A FULL LINE OF RUB-IN CREAMS FOR THE FLIGHT PATTERN YOU DESIRE...

WINGBAT'S EAGLE SOAR

WINGBAT'S PELICAN SEA DIVE

WINGBAT'S BUZZARD CIRCLE

WINGBAT'S HUMMING BIRD BUZZ ABOUT

WINGBAT'S CANADA GOOSE WATER SKIMMING

WINGBAT'S OWL FLY BY NIGHT

Rub in our miracle cream each night by moonlight. By morning wings will have grown! It takes only ten short weeks until they are ready for flight! Follow the *Easy-Step-By-Step Home Study Manual* and you will take off!

Get the whole set! The first 3 suckers to order will receive: ALL-WEATHER flying gear and goggles, PLUS

WARNING: WINGBAT'S wings do NOT come off! What you do with them after they sprout is YOUR problem!!

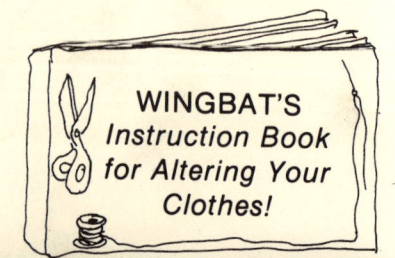

WINGBAT'S Instruction Book for Altering Your Clothes!

NOAHZARK is a unique collecting club!

There's only one Noah!

JOIN NOAHZARK

Each month you will receive not one but TWO exotic animals DELIVERED TO YOUR DOOR! Just circle 11 choices (the twelfth is a mystery duo surprise), and send in your membership application *today!*

Lion

Ostrich

Rhinoceros

Iguana

Platypus

White Elephant

Walrus

Great White Shark

Lovebirds

King & Queen Kong

Bedbug

Pterodactyl

Boa Constrictor

Extra charge for housebroken animals.

The first 100 new members will receive absolutely FREE a peewee size bottle of PEUEWEEEE, the powerful skunk perfume.

page 35

page 36

A Mirth EXCLUSIVE

from the year 8419
brought back via

FANTAZZ

the magic Fird Brame...

8419 MOON NEWS

Control Lab Says Pollution Crisis Temporary

A spokesperson for the Moon Pollution Control Laboratories said today that the current crisis is only temporary.

LAST MOON WHALE IS DEAD!

Last night the last Moon whale died. The species can now sadly be added to the long list of extinct Moon creatures. Whales were first brought to the Moon from Earth in 3254, and thrived until recently.

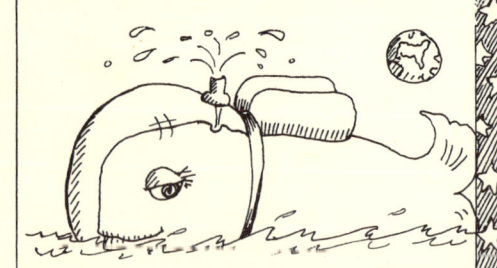

Last Moon whale as seen last year.

CANAL PLEA

The Moon Irrigation Committee has once again asked that garbage not be thrown into the canals.

The Irrigation Committee got on bended knee to make their plea.

THE LARGEST MAP IN THE GALAXY

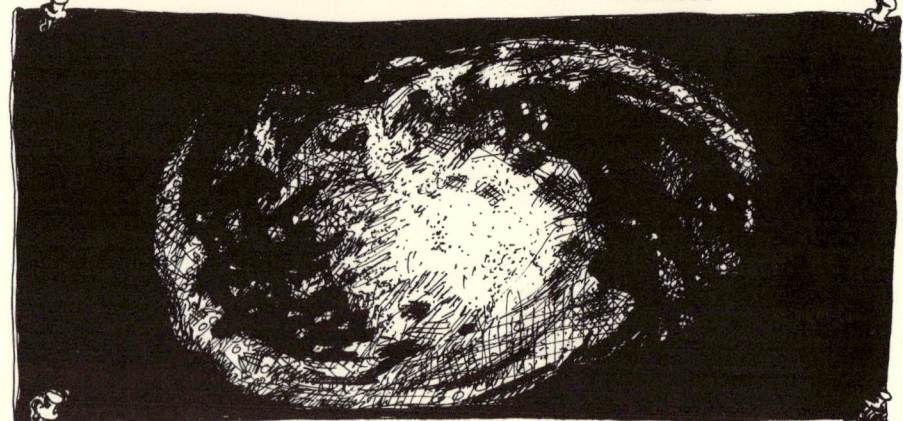

Now being sold by the Incredible Offer Company. Sales Limited to one map per planet, satellite, or asteroid. Map measures 100,000 light years in diameter.

COME TO EARTH

Come to the GREEN planet.
Get away from the dirt,
the pollution,
the crowding,
the dangers of MOON life.
... to the planet that has not been ruined!

page 37

Pelican

Carpenter Ants

Bedbug

Bookworm

Nightmare   Daymare

Frogmen

Crane

Gypsy Moth

Queen Bee & Monarch Butterfly

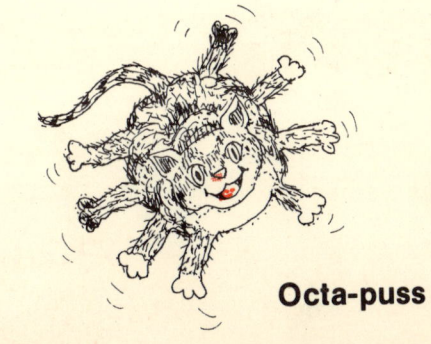

Octa-puss

page 38

Try this for real!

SNOWONDERS!

Forget those tired old snowmen. Make...

Snowwoman

Snowshoes

Snow Goose

Snowsuit

Snowplow

Whatever you make can be small enough to hold in your hand or keep on your window ledge, OR large enough that you'll need 20 people to help. Get someone with a snowplow to give you an enormously high pile of snow to make the *real* ABOMINABLE SNOWMAN!

Use hands, shovels, small boards to pack down the snow.

Use a wet sponge to smooth it. Pour water on it for interesting (but unpredictable) effects.

Optional Decorate with color. Mix food coloring in buckets of water and paint with brushes or sponges.
Decorate with stuff. Use anything the snow won't ruin—old clothes, twigs, branches, rocks, pebbles, sand, vegetables, and fruits.

Snow Vase

Snowmobile

Dress warmly, and have extra gloves!

Snow Maz

SPURTS

page 39

A Mirth Close-up

Track shoe track

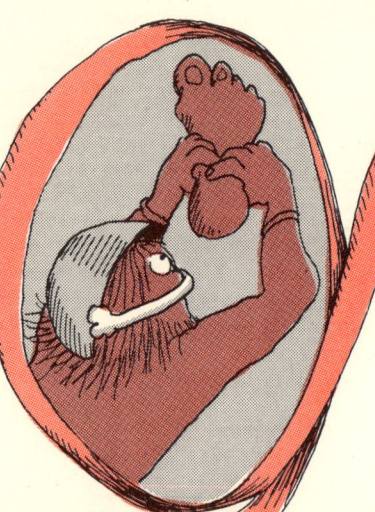

THE ILLUSTRATED Never-Before-Told HISTORY of SPORTS

FOOTBALL

was originally played with real feet, but it was so difficult to get a foot to play with, that other objects were used, and the ball gradually evolved into its present form.

BOWLING

is an ancient game handed down from the Howling tribe. It was first played before breakfast, using primitive cereal bowls. The Howlings would roll their bowls down a path trying to knock over a cereal box. Whoever was successful got to eat that morning.

SOCCER

was an early form of boxing. Once a year women would gather and run through the streets punching men in the nose. Back then the game was called *sock-him*. The men retaliated by playing *sock-her*. Fortunately, people now use a ball.

HORSESHOES

originated with the Nordic tribes known for their incredible strength. Their favorite pastime was lacing their own boots onto their horses' feet, whirling the horses in the air, and heaving them huge distances. As the Norse people traveled, they found that no one else would play with them, so they kept making the game easier and easier.

STAY IN SHAPE BUT NOT AWAKE
EXERCISE BED

Climb into the **STAY IN SHAPE BUT NOT AWAKE EXERCISE BED** as you would any other bed. Fasten your arms, legs, hands, and feet into the comfortable grippers. Set dials for desired degree of fitness and sport. Press start button, and go to sleep. When you begin dreaming, you activate the exerciser, and you're off on a restful, no work program that will have you ready for the next day's sport.

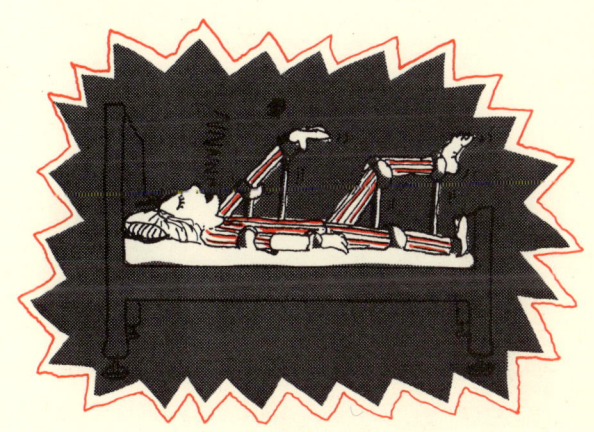

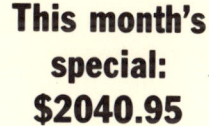

This month's special: $2040.95

Dials include: Football, Basketball, Baseball, Gymnastics, and Soccer.
Fitness control: beginner, amateur, olympic, pro.

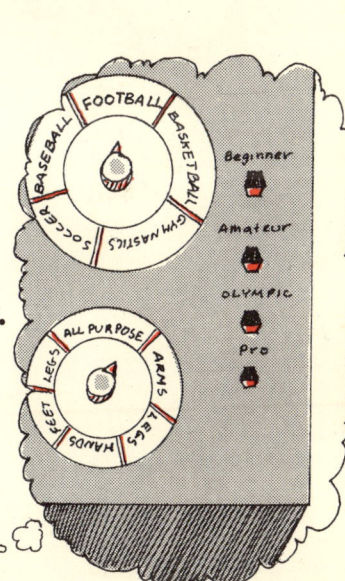

DOCTOR SOUL'S ALL PURPOSE HAT SOCKS

Don't you just hate dressing and undressing? At last... DOCTOR SOUL's ALL PURPOSE HAT SOCKS have solved this problem.
Hat socks also heal blisters and head bumps!

page 41

A-DOO-DAH! RUNNING SHOES

When you race with these the crowds will cheer: *A DOO DAH! A DOO DAH!*

Complete with extra soft cushions, racing stripe, and tiny jet engines in the soles and heels to give you that extra speed you've come to know as A-DOO-DAH!

Special attachments available for converting to mountain climbing shoes.

LEAVES OTHER BRANDS BEHIND!

BOWLING RECORDS — INFLATABLE

Listen to your ball while you wait your turn on the lane. Your friends will be green with envy as you dance to the sound of your bowling ball.

3 handy finger soles!

DOWN on DOWN???

GENUINE ARMADILLO GLUFF ALL-WEATHER GEAR

ONE SIZE FITS ALL—just adjust the individual plates. **COLORS:** natural, dayglow orange, ecology green, and filthy mud.

page 43

Now at last you can bring your pet on camping trips with worry-free **PETtents**

real petpleezers!

Shaped like a dog . . . for a dog. Available in small, medium, and **enormous**. Send for free color brochure of other PETtent Products.

- PUPglider
- PUPtents
- PUPcamper
- PARAtent
- PUPdingy
- KITtent
- GUPtent

THE 38-64-87 HIKE HELMET

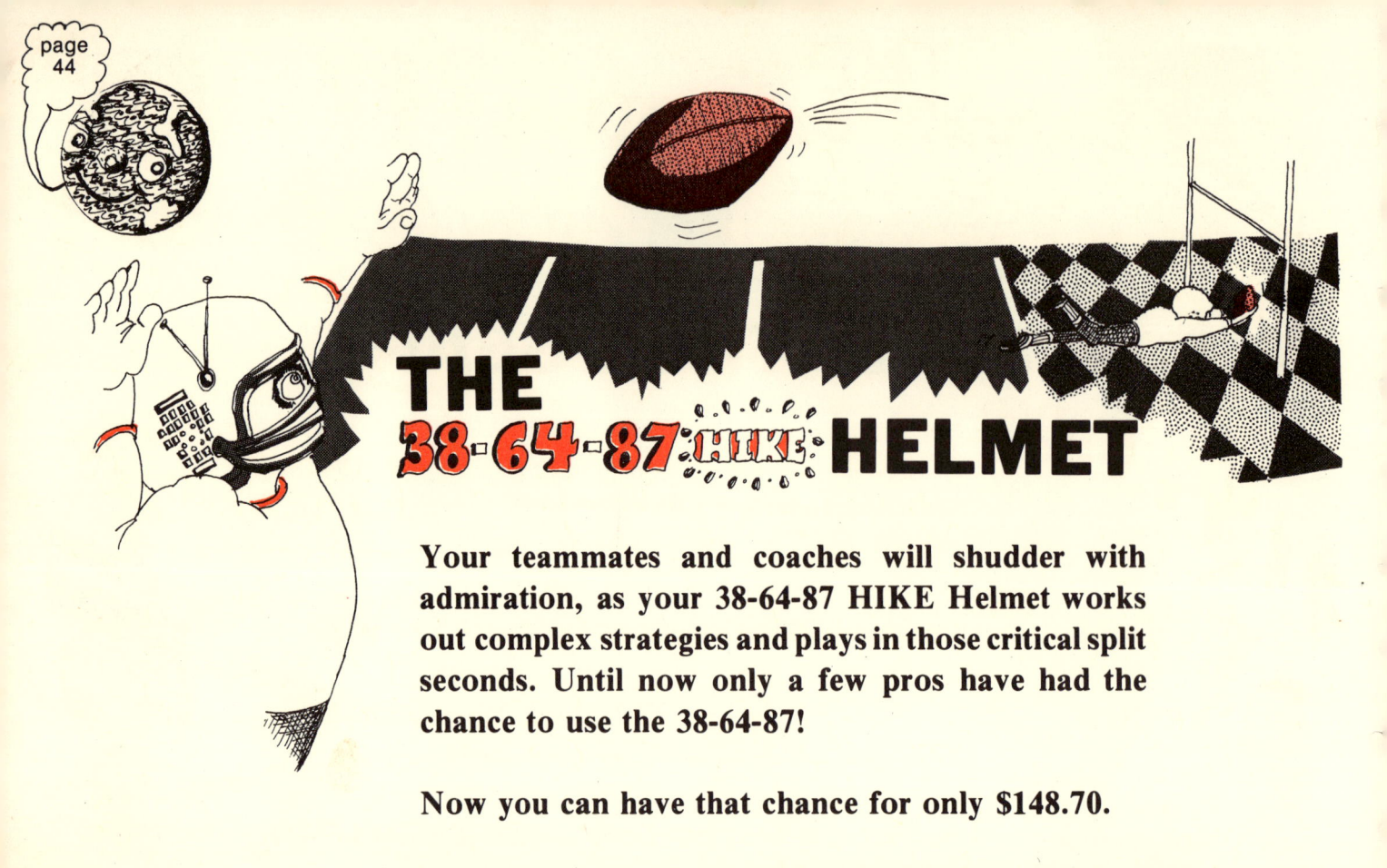

Your teammates and coaches will shudder with admiration, as your 38-64-87 HIKE Helmet works out complex strategies and plays in those critical split seconds. Until now only a few pros have had the chance to use the 38-64-87!

Now you can have that chance for only $148.70.

Guaranteed to get you out of the second string and off the bench!

The only computerized football helmet... technology at its utmost, working for you on the field!

Limpid's Program of complete BODY BUILDING

takes only eight hours ...
muscles overnight JUST where you want them!

Limpid's Program works for pets, too!

THE belchee! SEED COMPANY

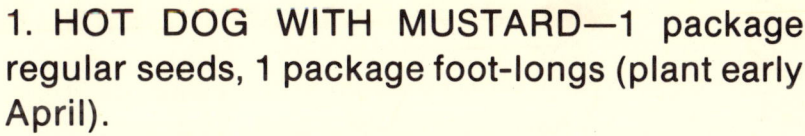

INTRODUCES

BALL GAME Seed Packet Sampler:

1. HOT DOG WITH MUSTARD—1 package regular seeds, 1 package foot-longs (plant early April).

2. ROLL SEEDS—specify toasted or plain.

3. ASSORTED SODA SEEDS—black cherry, orange, cola, and NEW root beer.

4. For the first time ever—ICE CREAM SANDWICH SEEDS.

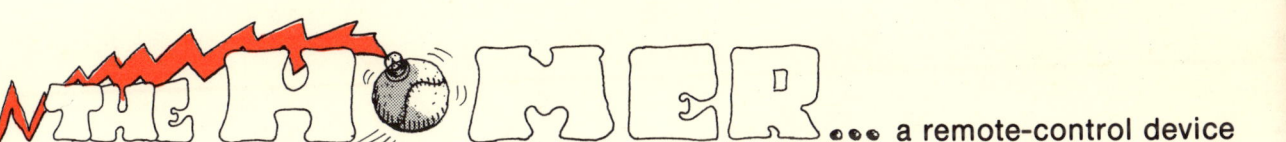

THE HOMER... a remote-control device

THE HOMER
SISTER BUG
MINI-SISTER BUG

Tuck it in your ear, put the sister bug onto ANY playing ball, and project your thought waves!
Basketballs come to you!
Footballs soar over goalposts!
Baseballs jet out of stadiums!
Hockey pucks obey your commands!
Mini-sister bug available for Ping-Pong and golf balls.

Batteries are not included.

page 46

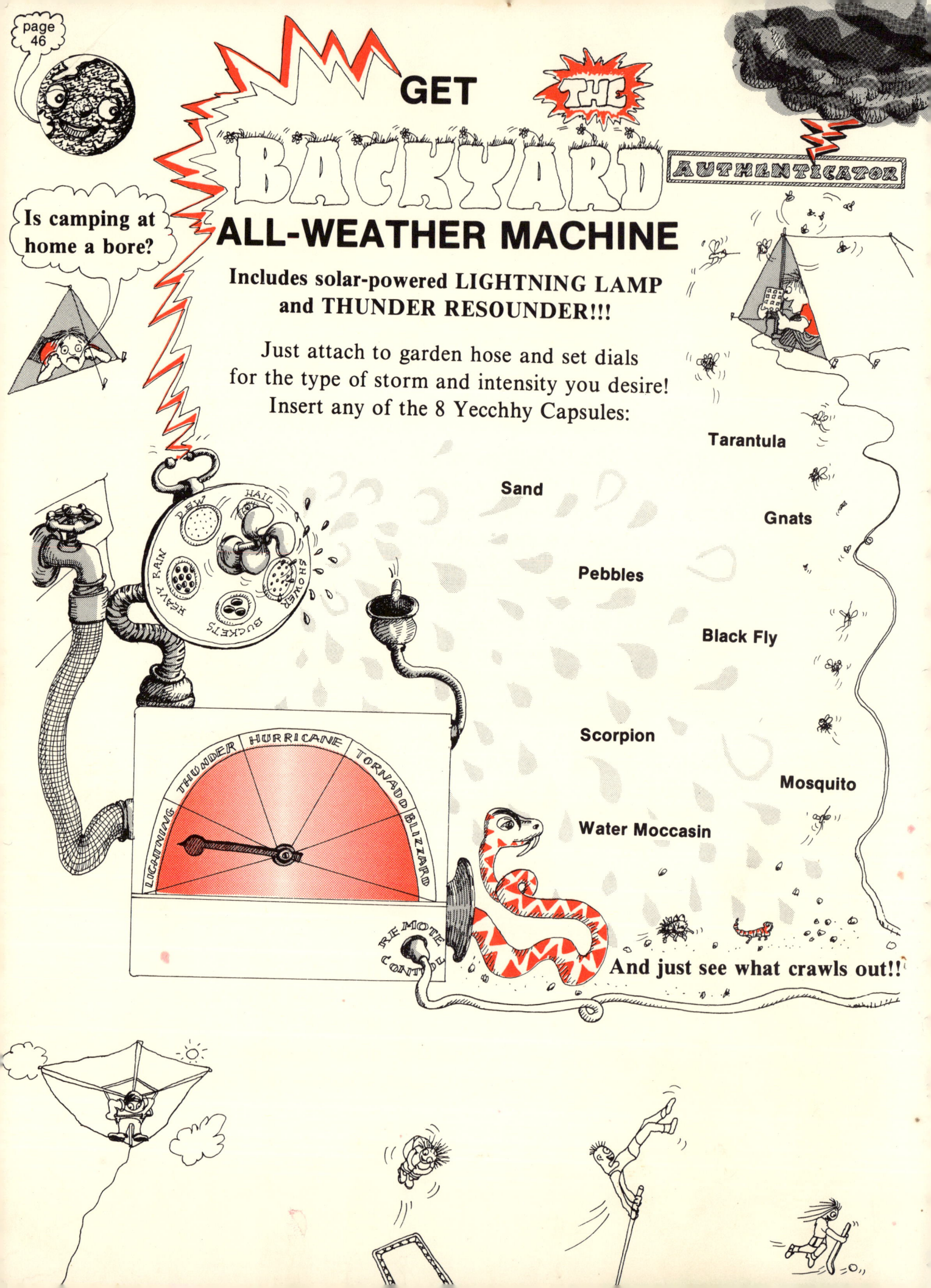

Is camping at home a bore?

GET THE BACKYARD AUTHENTICATOR
ALL-WEATHER MACHINE

Includes solar-powered LIGHTNING LAMP and THUNDER RESOUNDER!!!

Just attach to garden hose and set dials for the type of storm and intensity you desire! Insert any of the 8 Yecchhy Capsules:

- Tarantula
- Sand
- Gnats
- Pebbles
- Black Fly
- Scorpion
- Mosquito
- Water Moccasin

And just see what crawls out!!

Start your own TRAINED WORM SCHOOL

Beginners' Kit includes:
2 starter worms
Handy instruction booklet
One week supply of worm food

OR

Deluxe Kit includes:
8 starter worms
Handy instruction booklet
One year supply worm food
Worm size blackboard and chalk
Worm grade book and report cards
Worm diplomas
Easy-to-assemble advertising signs and roadside stand

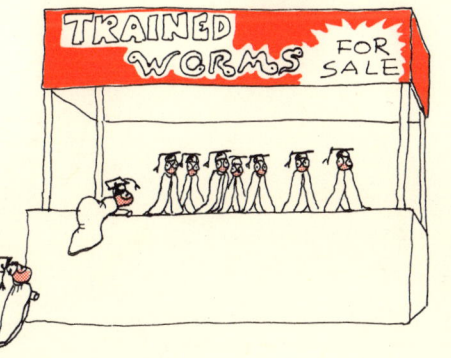

No ordinary offer!! Sell the most unusual and prized trained worms! Success guaranteed when you follow the worm school training manual! The worms you choose to graduate will catch fish without fail. They will learn to play tunes that have delighted fish for ages. Each worm will study and master 65 fish calls that will lure the most stubborn fish. In two short months your worms will graduate and bring you FANTASTIC PROFITS!

The smartest worms bait themselves!
Don't worry about dirt . . . these worms bathe twice a day!
Don't delay! Act now! HURRY!
Don't wiggle away from this spectacular offer!
For dumber worms, get special Tutor Worms—only 69¢ each.

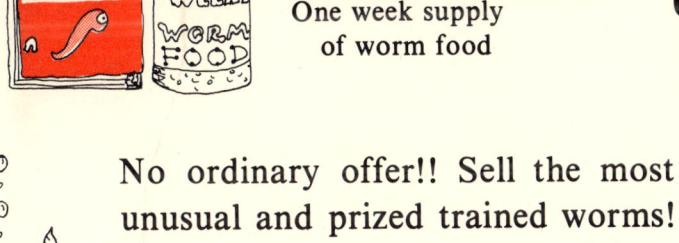

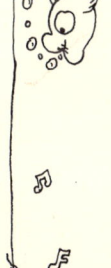

GAMES FOR GOLIATH

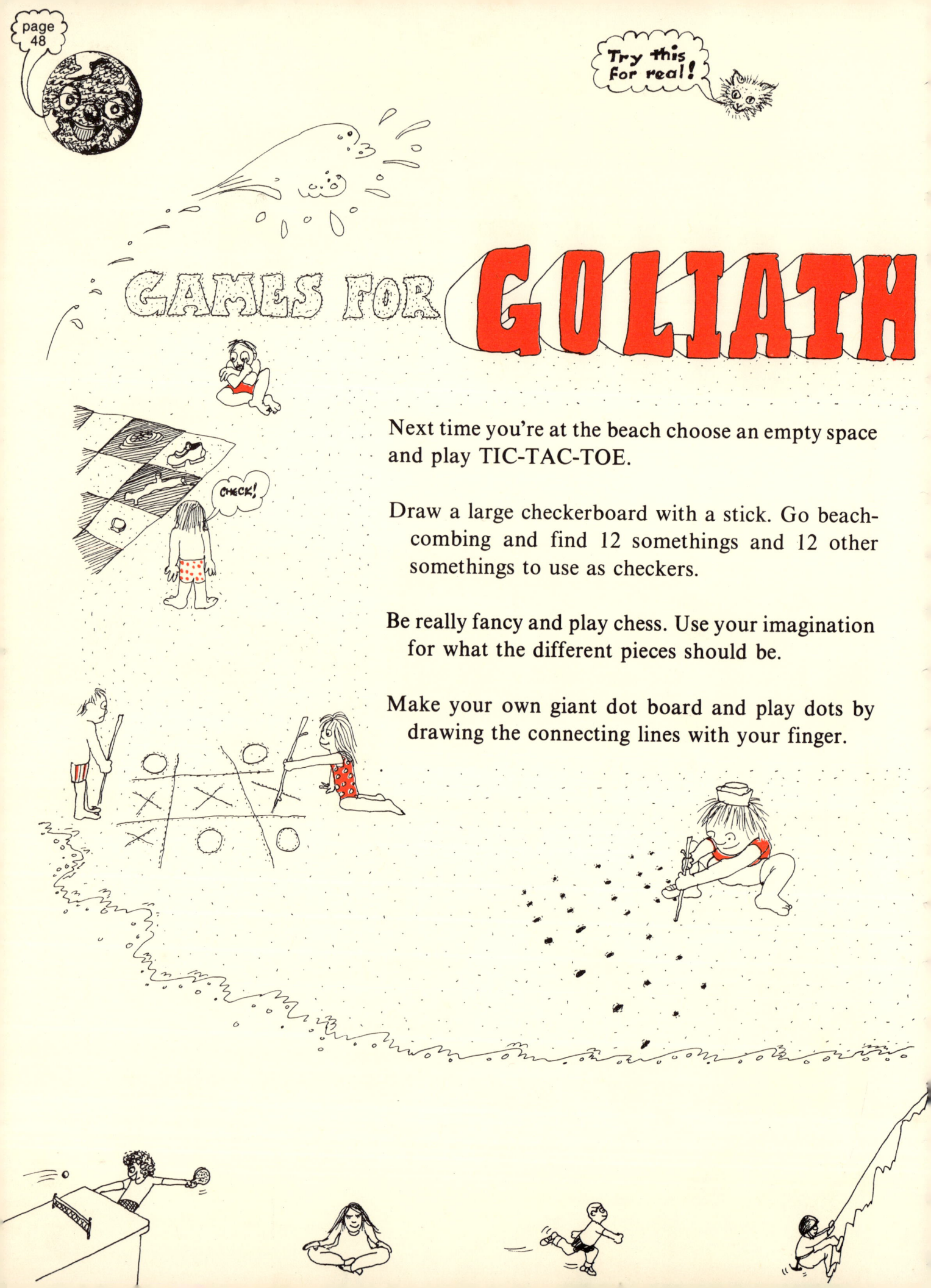

Next time you're at the beach choose an empty space and play TIC-TAC-TOE.

Draw a large checkerboard with a stick. Go beach-combing and find 12 somethings and 12 other somethings to use as checkers.

Be really fancy and play chess. Use your imagination for what the different pieces should be.

Make your own giant dot board and play dots by drawing the connecting lines with your finger.

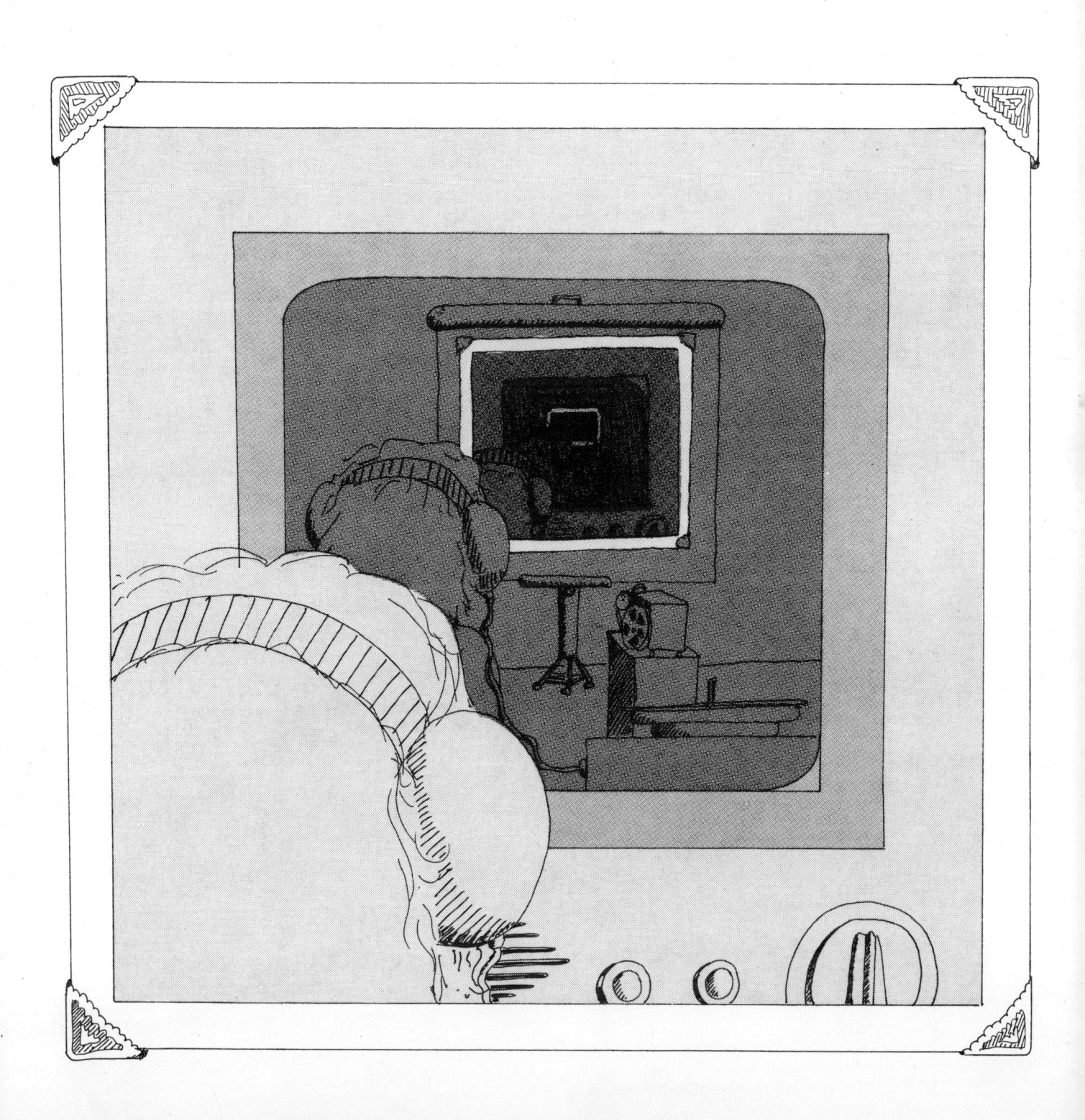

MIXED-UP MEDIA

page 50

**Do you know your ACB's?
Do you have a hold on your handle?
This book may change YOUR life!**

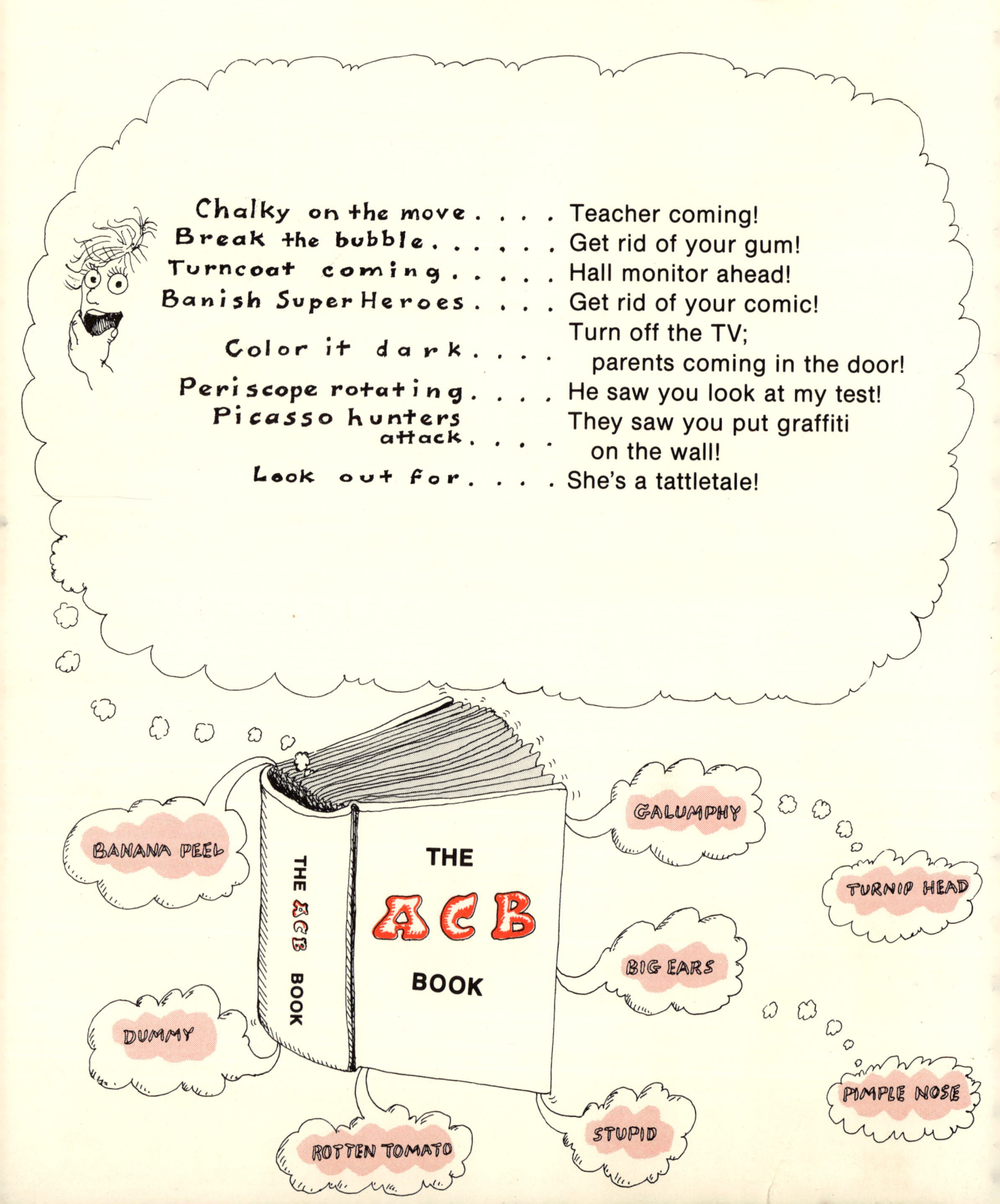

Chalky on the move....	Teacher coming!
Break the bubble.....	Get rid of your gum!
Turncoat coming....	Hall monitor ahead!
Banish Super Heroes...	Get rid of your comic!
Color it dark....	Turn off the TV; parents coming in the door!
Periscope rotating....	He saw you look at my test!
Picasso hunters attack....	They saw you put graffiti on the wall!
Look out for....	She's a tattletale!

THE ACB BOOK

BANANA PEEL
GALUMPHY
TURNIP HEAD
BIG EARS
PIMPLE NOSE
STUPID
ROTTEN TOMATO
DUMMY

Be the undercover agent in your house!

GET Bedtime PARTY BOX

when you're alone or at a party!

It's a miniature media center designed to slip under your covers.

Comes complete with:

Earphones,
micro-mini TV,
Quad system
 (deluxe tuner, turntable,
 and speakers),
5 miniature records of
 your choosing,
AM/FM radio,
reading light,
snack cabinet*

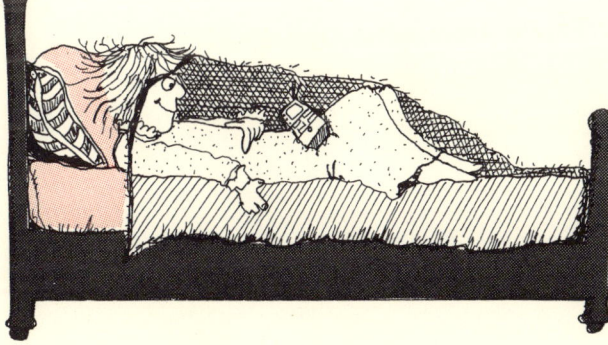

*with complimentary sampler of **BEDTIME SNACKS**— the quiet, crunchless, slurpless, nighttime foods!

BEDTIME PARTY BOX casts NO light! Guaranteed not to be detected!

page 51

RADI-OAP

The Only Disposable Radio-Soap-On-A-Rope

Makes washing your ears as pleasant as possible.

Warning: As **RADI-OAP** gets smaller, it gets harder and harder to change the stations.

IT FLOATS... IT SINGS!

FABULOUS MAGAZINE OFFER!

Subscribe to ONE for just 32 years and get the other 2 absolutely FREE! Each exciting issue filled with projects, puzzles, stories, games, and thrilling essay contests you are guaranteed not to win!

**for just $10.00 each
or get all 3 for $47.50**

COCK-A-ROACH
THE MAGAZINE for SMARTER KIDS

This Month: Making Life Miserable for Your Brothers and Sisters...

NEXT MONTH:

Clothes You & Your Pet Can Wear

The History of Popsicle Sticks named for their inventor, Pop Sickle

NEXT MONTH:

How to Get Your Family to Pay Attention to You: Dress up like a cabbage, with detailed step-by-step instructions...

FULL page color-in poster of a mosquito biting an arm...

Children's Ragazine
HOLIDAY ISSUE

3 Boring Stories Every Month that we know you'll L♥VE to read!

page 53

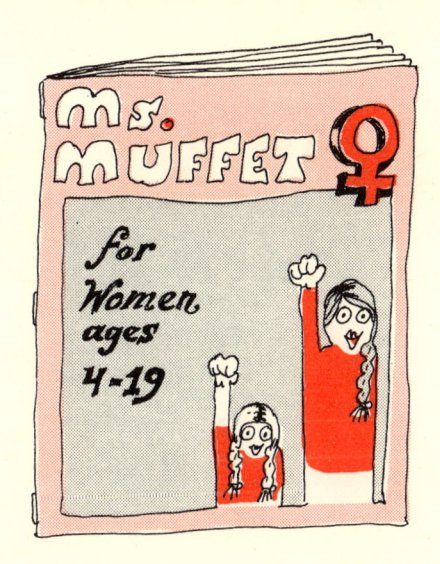

NEXT MONTH:

19, the last teen—
worse than they say...

Big dates—Going out
with basketball players...

Hollywood stars talk about
SUPER POWERS they wish they had...

Feel silly with your old walkie-talkie? Throw it away!
Burn those tin cans tied with string!
Put your CB in the garbage disposal.
Here comes

SPI

the Super Perception Increaser

**SPI is *the* telepathy set!
SPI reads minds for you!**

Tune into your parents' thoughts, your teacher's plans, your brother's and sister's schemes! Beam messages to whomever you wish! Tiny receiver snaps onto a strand of hair just above your ear. Transmitter fits nicely between your teeth. Antennae hang invisibly from your eyelids.

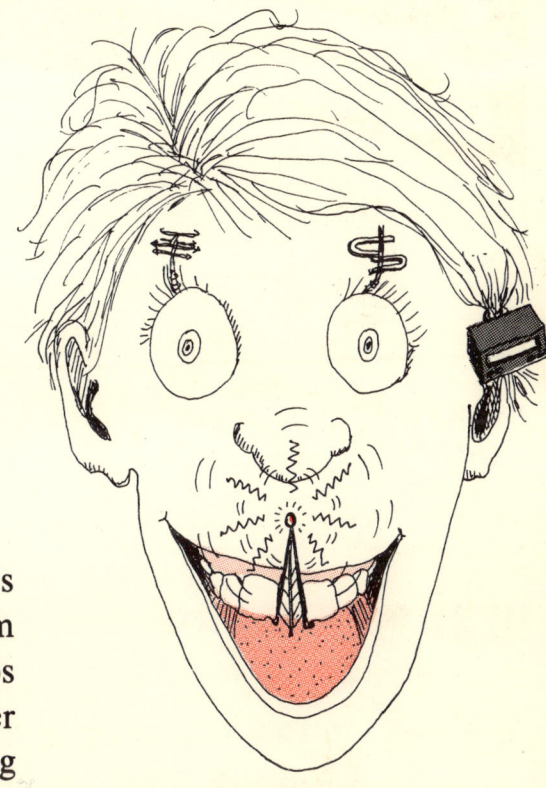

CAUTION: We are reading your mind right now! The last 18 people who didn't order SPI have disappeared!

Send away for a FREE TRIAL offer now!

Send away for a FREE TRIAL offer now!

Send away for a FREE TRIAL offer now!

**This month only: Buy 2 SPI's
and receive a free levitation transformer.**

(Offer limited to participating dealers.)

page 54

WIN $$$$$ VALUABLE PRIZES!
BY SELLING GREETING CARDS.

Learn how to bother all your friends, relatives, neighbors, teachers, and even strangers on the street!!!!!!

People will run when they see you coming, as you work your way to winning these fabulous bonus prizes.

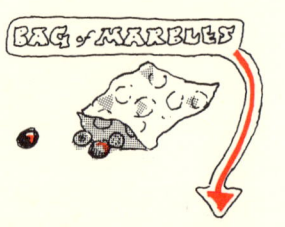

10 SPEED RACING BIKE — sell just 2,840,137 boxes

CB RADIO — sell 1,942,003 boxes

BAG of MARBLES — sell just 10 boxes

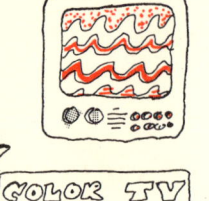

PENCIL — sell 1 box

CROSS COUNTRY Ski Equipment — sell 4,006,294 boxes

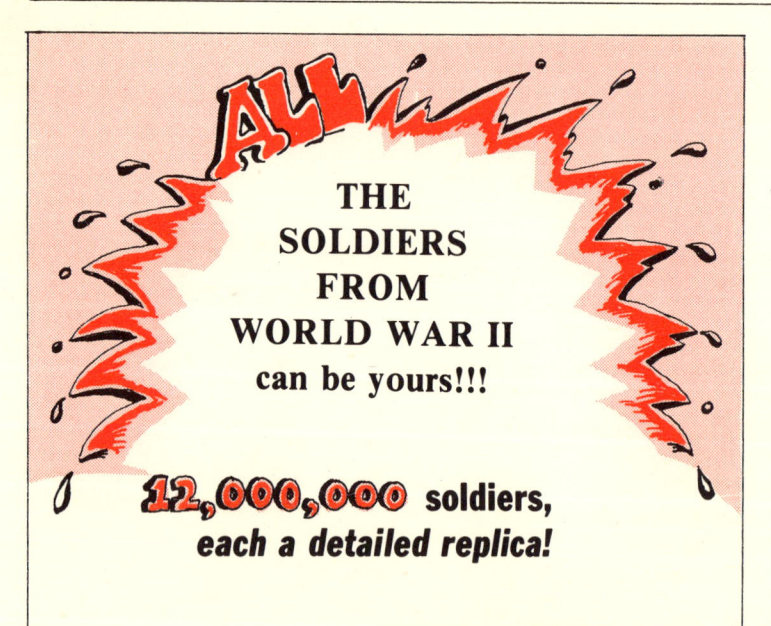

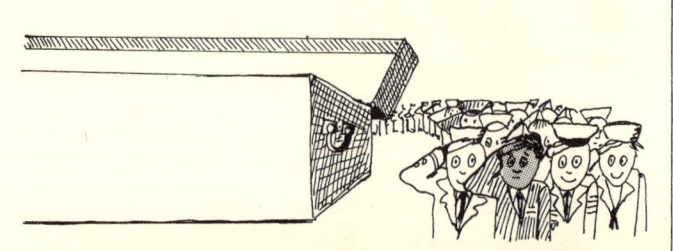

COLOR TV — sell 3,487,621 boxes

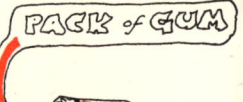

PACK of GUM — sell 3 boxes

DECK of CARDS — sell just 25 boxes

ALL THE SOLDIERS FROM WORLD WAR II can be yours!!!

12,000,000 soldiers, each a detailed replica!

Set comes complete with its own chest; chest stands 3 inches (7.6 cm) high and 50 miles (80.5 km) long.

EVERY STAMP EVER MINTED

backed with spearmint-flavored glue...

AN UNBELIEVABLE OFFER!

ALSO: EVERY COIN EVER MINTED!

You're probably saying to yourself right at this very moment, "That's IMPOSSIBLE!" but these unique coin and stamp collections are BACKED by the president of our company.

Company President

MAGIT-HAPPEN

Practical Magic Tricks for Daily Living

page 55

Want to see your teacher's mouth hang open?

Amaze your friends and make parents or teachers disappear!

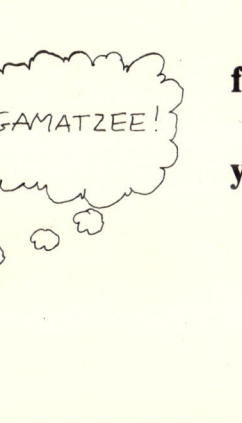

Make an elephant appear in class!

Pull quarters from your nose just when you need them!

GAMATZEE!

Reduce a bully to the size of your little toe!

GAMATZEE!

Bored on family trips? Change the car into a giant horse!

MAGIT-HAPPEN supplies you with:

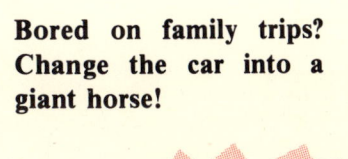

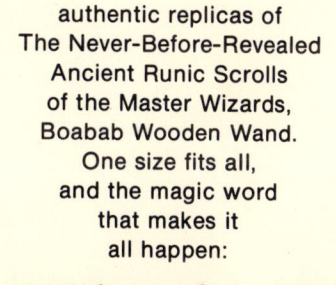

authentic replicas of The Never-Before-Revealed Ancient Runic Scrolls of the Master Wizards, Boabab Wooden Wand. One size fits all, and the magic word that makes it all happen:

GAMATZEE!

Brothers and sisters hassling you? Change them into toads!

GAMATZEE!

Introductory kit $3.46
Spell Reverser kit $2,531.99!

page 56

BLOOD & GUTS MAGAZINE

A BLOOD & GUTS EXCLUSIVE

Midnight on WEIRD ISLAND
The world's only Cemetery Amusement Park

by Jack T. Ripper, Jr.

The deserted church at the gateway to Weird Island chimed 13 times, as I entered into a night I would never forget. I bought the deluxe book of Cryptickets from a devil and was rowed across a murky river moat on a flimsy raft by a troll. I spent the entire night, until the first light of dawn, at the Cemetery Amusement Park, going on every ride, touring each exhibit, and sampling all the strange foods at the many bizarre refreshment stands.

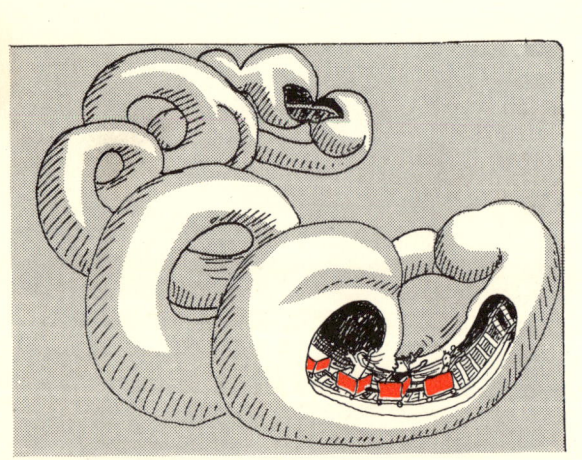

The **Wild Scorpion** was terrorific! Fast and frightening, the track twists and whips through dark tunnels and passageways in a ten-story mausoleum.

I climbed on my broomstick at the **Witches' Broomousel,** and was carried higher and higher as I spiraled around a full moon with the black cat organ cackling and shrieking in my ears.

I entered the **Mummy's Maze,** an ancient Egyptian Pyramid. Once in the tombs, I had to find my way through the maze of hallways, some narrow, some high, some so low I had to wriggle on my belly. When I reached the center the Mummy greeted me and handed me an end of its wrapping. The Mummy ran off, leaving a trail of gauze to follow, until I finally exited and came face to face with the horrifying contents of what lay beneath the layers of gauze. It sent chills through my bones.

Volume 13   Issue 13

At the **Dracula Shooting Range,** the guns have silver bullets.

Try to walk from one end of the **Graveyard Outdoor Fun House** to the other without your hair turning white! Every kind of ghost, goblin, and ghoul attacks. The Zombie followed this reviewer slowly, but relentlessly, as I tried to get to safety.

Mad Scientist's Lab—help stitch Frankenstein together, or make your own gruesome sundae.

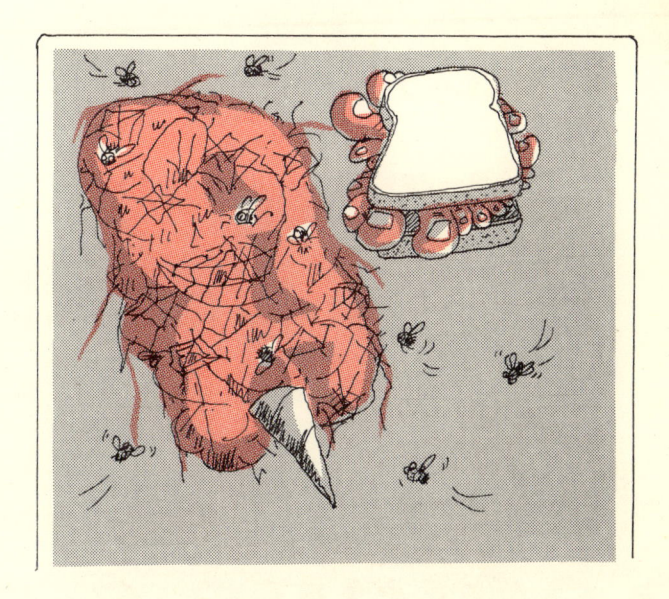

Don't miss the Jekyll & Hyde sodas, Sloppy Toes sand-witches smothered in Sorcerers' Sauce, and the Blood Burgers. Candy Cobwebs take some getting used to; flies tend to get stuck in them.

Souvenirs include batboy dolls, authentic evil-eyeball key rings, claw slippers, full-moon balloons, and werewolf hair tonic for face and head.

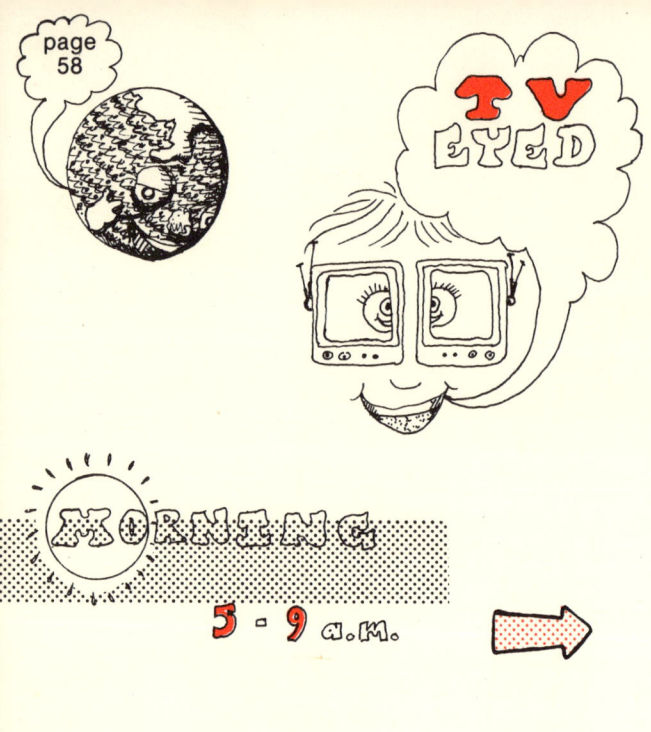

Coming soon... to your area
KBC — Kid Broadcasting Company
the Brand New Kid Network!

Programs made just for you, 24 hours a day, every day! Say goodbye to just Saturday morning, to a few after-school specials, and to an occasional show you like...Say hello to KBC with *your* shows, anytime you feel like watching...

MORNING

5 - 9 a.m. → **Current Events**—morning talk show with news, weather, and The Homework Helper (call-in questions, panel of experts will answer).

9 - 2:30 a.m. → **The Home Sick Show**—games, stories, cartoons, and Dr. Fakeit with tips on how to stay out at least one extra day.

AFTERNOON

2:30 - 5 p.m. → **TGSO** — Thank Goodness School's Over — come home, get a snack, put your feet up, and relax with TGSO after a hard day in the classroom. Pure enjoyment. No learning sneaked in!

EVENING

5 - 7 p.m. → **Play with Your Food**—suppertime entertainment specials.

7 - 7:30 p.m. → **Gnews and Weather UPDATE**—starring Guesso.

7:30 - 8 p.m. → **How to Live with Your Parents**—advice, tips, and the latest research findings.

8 - 9 p.m. → **KIDD, Detective**—world's youngest private eye, who keeps an extra eye in his pocket.

9 - 5 p.m. → **All-Nite Movies**—send in your requests.

☆ SPECIAL ☆

Sunday night 7:30-10 p.m. on KBC
MOM 'n' DAD—a true documentary about parents today, and how they use their power. Get them to go out! You must see this show ALONE, and uninterrupted!

X-TRAORDINARY

TV POP — NOW eat the corn while you watch the corn and never have to leave the room with this Xtraordinary TV-Popcorn Attachment— Butter Melter not included.

Saturday afternoon at the MOVIES

Wouldn't it be nice if . . .

. . . the refreshment stand sold hamburgers, hot dogs, and hush puppies?

. . . the candy counter would deliver to your seat?

. . . there were places to put your feet up?

. . . no one over 18 was admitted?

. . . ushers didn't have flashlights?

. . . there was always a door prize?

. . . they showed quadruple features?

. . . they ran the same movies they show at night?

PHONY PHOTOGRAPHY

Try this for real!

Have a friend stand on a hillside; have another friend stand in front. Line them up in the view finder of your camera so that one friend *seems* to be standing on the other's head or in the other's hands.

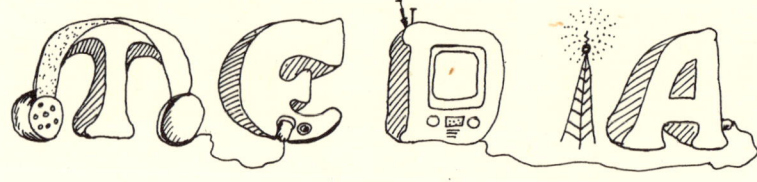

MIXED-UP MEDIA

For a different experience:

Watch TV with the sound off and the radio or stereo on.

Get 2 TV's together on different channels, one with sound off, one with sound on.

Turn 2 radios to different stations and put ear jacks in each ear. Try this with a stereo and a radio, too.

Dogs gobble CHOMPEES...

STUFF

page 61

page 62

GIANT EXPANDING Sloppy-Gloppy

ACCEPT NO IMITATIONS.

It's *DISGUSTING!*

Your parents will hate it!!!

Comes in 9 pastel colors
Non-toxic!
Non-removable!

Once you take it out of its container, SLOPPY-GLOPPY fills your room. Take it out of your room and it fills your apartment, your house! Let it outdoors and it may take over your town . . . and once on the loose, it may take over the world!! SLOPPY-GLOPPY is more than a toy; it's a disaster! Play with it once; that may be the last chance you have!!

BORED GAME

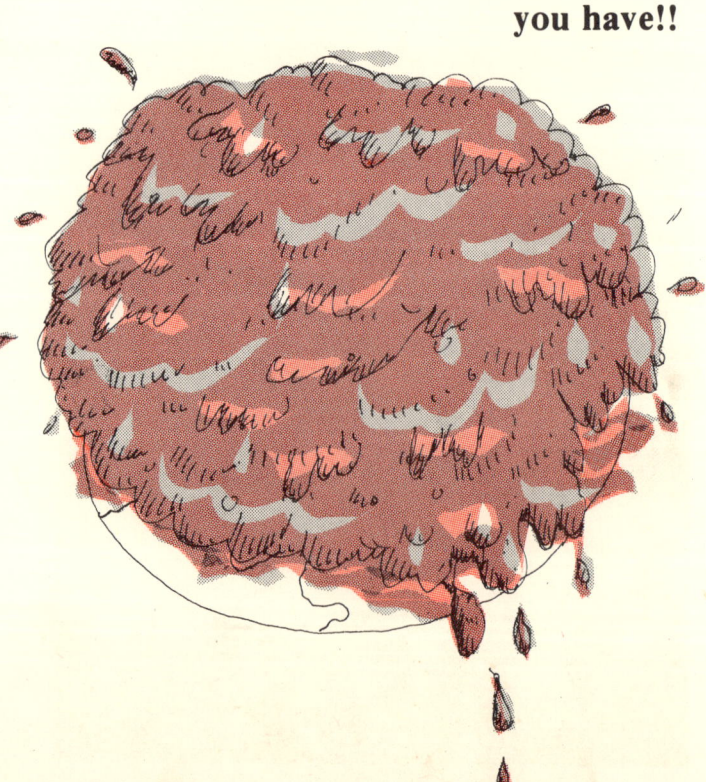

HO HUM

page 63

When you get tired of fixing up all those beautiful dolls, GET

OLD UGLY FACE

The only doll you can make UGLIER 100 different ways! With 8 special ugly make-down kits.

Depending on your mood, add:

MOLDY	MOLES
SCABBY	SCABS
POCKY	ACNE
BALD	SPOTS
WIGGLY	WARTS
PINK	PIMPLES

and
splotches,
stitches,
drooling switch,
nose runner,
tooth yellower,
and MUCH MUCH MORE!

PERFECT GIFTS FOR PARENTS & TEACHERS

WITH SEE-NO-EVIL GLASSES
your parents will laugh when the top falls off the saltshaker into your sister's food!

WITH HEAR-NO-EVIL EARRINGS
your teacher will never hear you whispering to your friend.

WITH SPEAK-NO-EVIL LIP BALM
no one can ever yell at you.

THE Whole Mirth RIP OFF AWARD

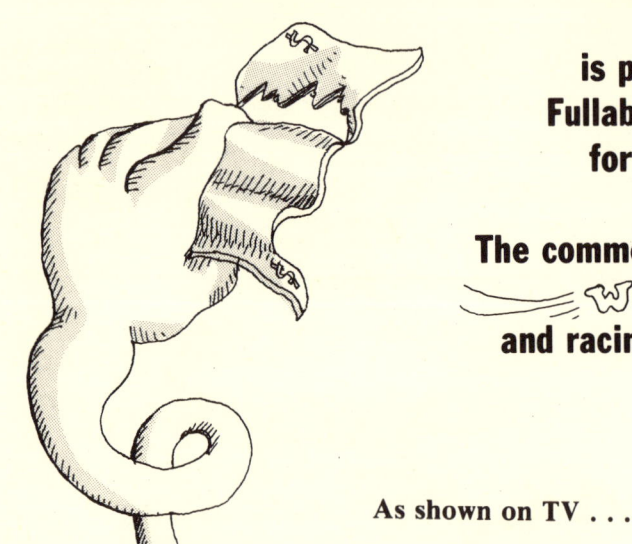

is presented this year to Fullabaloni Plastics Company for their dumb product, WHOOSH the Wonder Car. The commercial shows a boy sitting in WHOOSH and racing at the Indianapolis 500.

As shown on TV...

As it really is without trick photography!!!!!

It's not FAIR when...

You've mastered the jigsaw puzzle and there's just one piece missing!

The easy-to-assemble model takes eight days to put together and the instructions are printed in a foreign language!

The gum people put less and less in a package and all the cards are the same!

You send 25¢ and a self-addressed stamped envelope and the booklet never comes!

FANTAZZ

THE MAGIC FIRD BRAME

A TIME-THOUGHT PROJECTOR...

Hold FANTAZZ over any photo, comic, TV show, newspaper article, or book. Press suction button, and in a POOUF of smoke and less than twenty seconds, find yourself transported into the world of whatever you've put in FANTAZZ, THE MAGIC FIRD BRAME. Inner FIRD BRAME is fully adjustable to fit any picture.

Go anywhere! Anytime! Anyplace!

Visit faraway lands!

Share adventures with your favorite super hero!

Be a guest star on your favorite show!

Romp with dinosaurs!

Travel to your favorite time period!

Mr. Fixed-it-but-good shows you how to make STRING ART

You'll need 4 pieces of wood
hammer
nails
scissors
24 balls of string, twine, or yarn
white glue

page 66

AQUARIUM
JANUARY

Aquariums seek their own level. They fall for things hook, line, and sinker, and wear high rubber boots indoors. Their symbol is The Fish Tank.

PIES
FEBRUARY

Pies are sweet, but nutty as fruitcakes. They can be very flaky in the morning, but have a thick crust. Can be recognized by the scoop of vanilla ice cream they sometimes wear on their heads. Their symbol is Cherry Pie.

GUMINI
MAY

Hot-tempered; quick to blow up, but a Gumini will stick to you through thick and thin. Like to chew things up; make great dentists and collectors of trading cards. Symbol: The Pink Bubble.

CANOPENER
JUNE

People born under Canopener often go around in circles. They make terrific auto wreckers.

SCOREBOARDO
OCTOBER

People born under this sign have a great sense of team spirit. They cheer others on, and are very good with numbers. Favorite pastime: addition.

ZEBRA
SEPTEMBER

Zebras horse around a lot, and race through whatever they do. Favorite color: stripes. Favorite song: "Jail House Rock"

STEP 1
Lay boards out just so to form a square.

page 67

HAIRIES
MARCH
Don't lock horns with a Hairies. They rarely go out in the daytime and go crazy when there's a full moon. Symbol is The Werewolf.

SOARUS
APRIL
Soaruses never have their feet on the ground, and tend to look down on others. Especially good at hang gliding.
Favorite book: Jonathan Livingston Seagull.

TRIO
JULY
Trios make good one-person bands.
Favorite saying: "Three's company; two's a crowd!"

STOPGO
AUGUST
Stopgos change their minds often. They make excellent traffic officers.
Favorite game: red light-green light.
Motto: Walk don't walk.

CONTAGIOUS
NOVEMBER
Contagious is the sign of the runny nose. They eat too many cough drops but are very generous in passing things around, including their tissues.
Favorite plant: poison ivy.

POPCORN*
DECEMBER
Popcorns* are easy to butter up, and they tell the corniest jokes. Hang out in movie theaters.
Favorite food: salt.
Favorite job: Christmas tree decorator.

*(due to the movement for women's equality, this sign is being changed to Momandpopcorn.)

STEP 2
Hammer boards together at each corner.

MOTHER N'S WEATHER

PAINTS . . . . . Go On Like Magic

Dip in your brush and paint walls, ceilings, closets, even floors with the weather of your choice . . . 9 wayout colors to choose from. Get them all; be as changeable as the weather!

RAIN DROPS   CLOUDS WITH BLUE SKY   SLEET
SNOW FLAKES   CLOUDS WITH GRAY SKY
STARRY NIGHT   RAINBOW   "ATOMIC" HOLOCAUST
POLLUTION   AND THE BRAND NEW JUST DEVELOPED ➔ SIDEWALK SLUSH

STARRY NIGHT

RAINBOW mixed with CLOUDS WITH BLUE SKY

Most people can't tell weather paints from the real thing! With MOTHER N'S YOU CAN TOUCH THE SKY!!!!!!!!!!

STEP 3
Stand frame against a wall and hammer nails all the way around the frame.

STEP 4
Tie end of each ball of string onto a nail and begin winding the string to make your own masterpiece pattern.

FEELING LONELY? Need a new friend?

page 69

Get

PEN-PALS

The pen that's your friend when no else will be!

comes in 5 warm colors

Cheer-you-up Yellow
Share-your-sadness Blue
Non-envious Green
Doesn't-criticize-you Red
Helpful-and-generous Purple

TWO styles available! Ask for

MARK-HERS and **MARK-HIMS**

FELT TIPS HAVE FEELINGS TOO!

STEP 5

Forget this stupid project. It's the dumbest thing I ever saw!

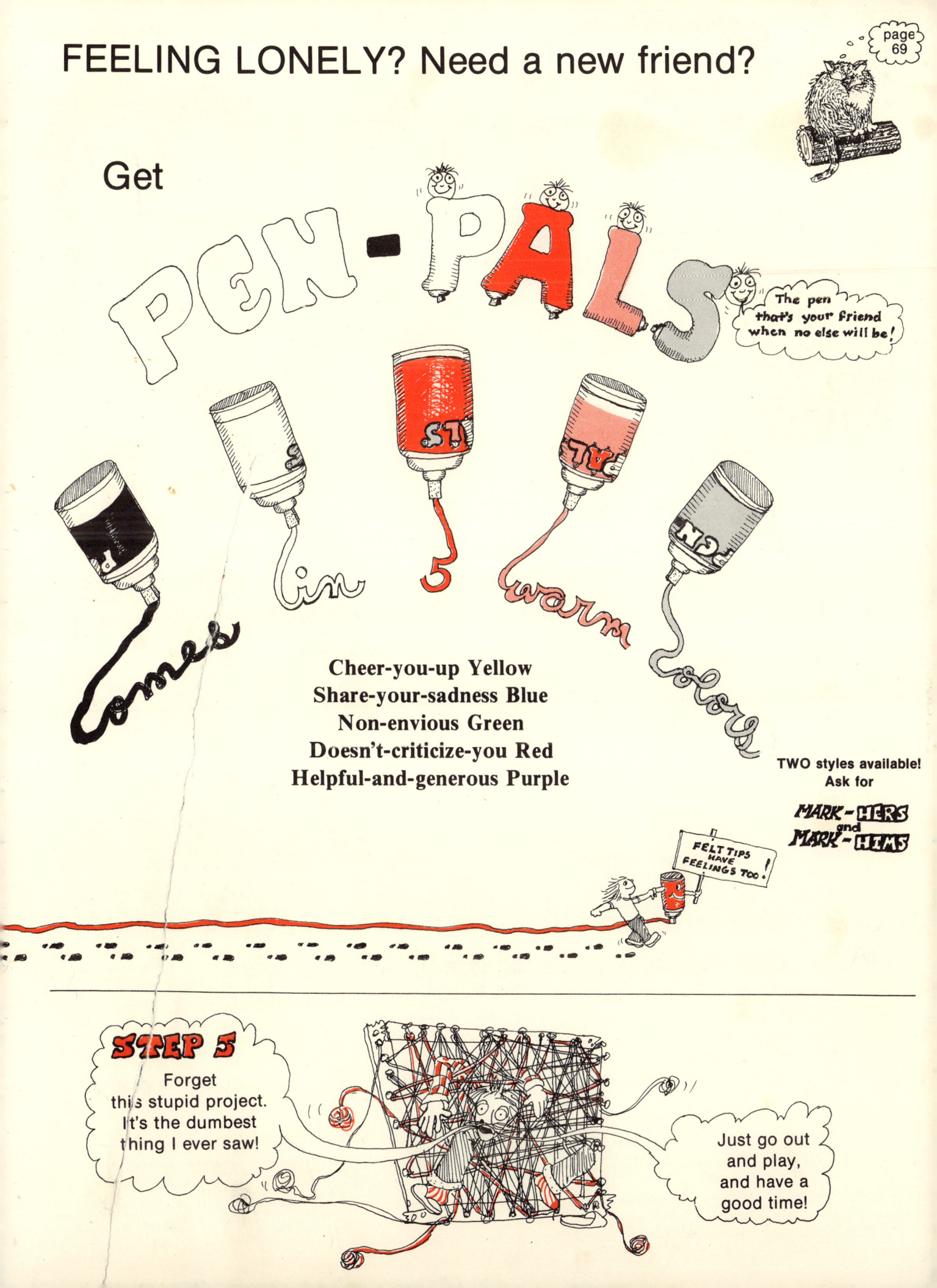

Just go out and play, and have a good time!

BLUE JEANIES
The Disposable Dungarees

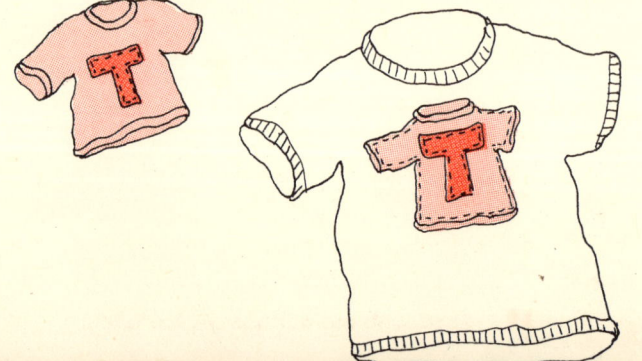

**Wear one pair for six months!
No need to take them off or ever change again!**

New magic formula and wonder fabric will please you and your mom. When BLUE JEANIES get dirty or torn just rub the sensitized brass-lamp-waist-snap and a new pair materializes on your body.

Old jeans are new again!

Buy 3 pairs and get your FREE

LIVING GARTER BELT

T-T-T-T-SHIRT

Try this for real!

Sew a cloth "T" onto a baby-sized T-shirt. Sew the baby T-shirt onto the front of your T-shirt. Wear it!

BLOW IT OUT AND MAKE A WISH!!

How many times have YOU heard *this*?
Wish it were true????
Well, it is. With

WARLOCK'S WISH CANDLES

YOUR wishes will come true!

Blow them all out in one breath, open your eyes, and . . .

ZAMMY

WARLOCK says:

The wish candle formula comes from an ancient diary of Merlin the Magician!

In the future watch for:
WARLOCK'S WISH Upon a Star ☆
WARLOCK'S WITCH WISH Bones
WARLOCK'S Working WISHing Well

Well, maybe . . . but they WORK!

CHEWIES ARTIFICIAL Orange TROUBLE BUBBLE GUMBLE

Chew it today, wear it tomorrow!

We process your chewed gum — INTO —

CUSTOM T-SHIRTS!

Cut out coupon and send 330 pounds (150 kg) of chewed GUMBLE along with $1.95 and coupon

to: CHEW-IT   Gumbleville, NY 00000

name _____
number of arm holes _____
number of head holes _____
address _____
one sticky size fits all with our miracle stretch fabric

ZOOPY LABELS

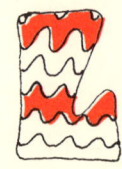

HOW TO HOLD ON TO YOUR STUFF AND HAVE FUN DOING IT!

Create your own individual labels by drawing, cutting, and pasting...

Draw comic balloons. Outline the balloon on paper, cut it out, and paste it on record albums, books, game boxes, anything you want labeled **YOURS!**

Write your own message:

Cut out a picture of a monster or draw your own.

Cut out words and letters from magazines and paste up your own fearsome message.

You can also buy pregummed labels in many colors.

LEARNIN'

page 73

Grilled
Cheese
Sandwich

A Mirth Close-up
The truth about school lunches

Spaghetti
and
Meatballs

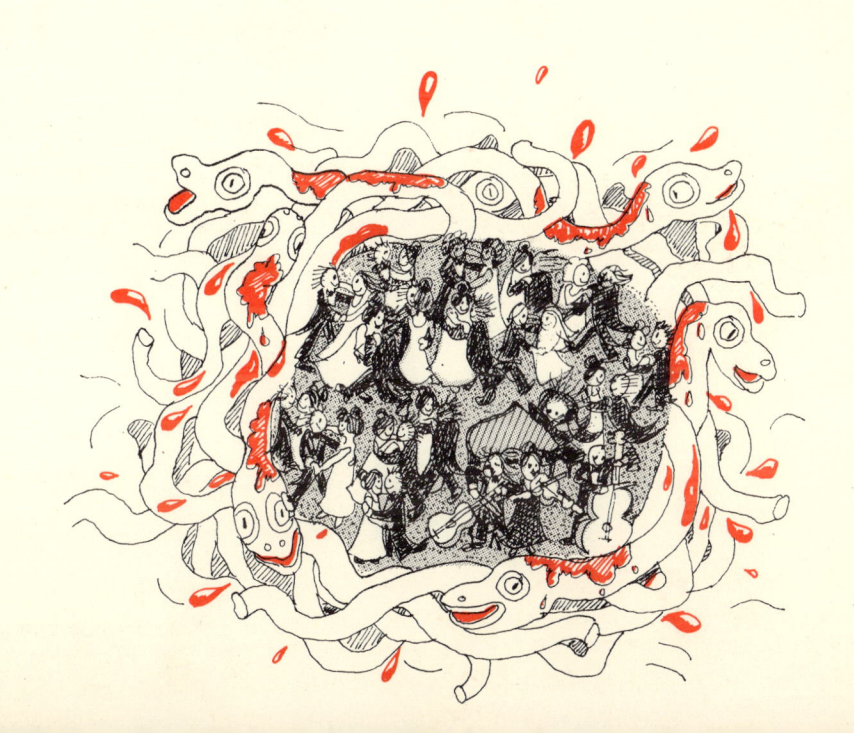

page 74

The Truth About the World ATLAST!

Who can remember where all those places are?
Answer: No one can! *(upside down)*

ATLAST! real ways to keep track of it all in the

All your questions answered ATLAST!

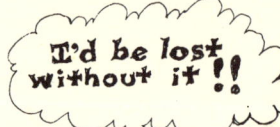

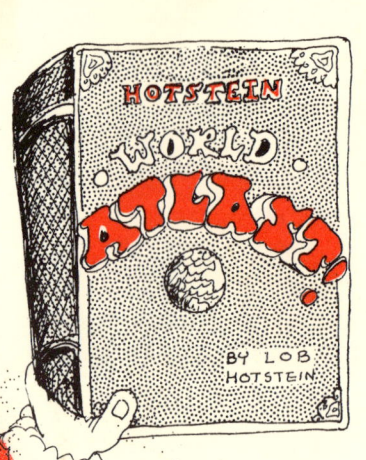

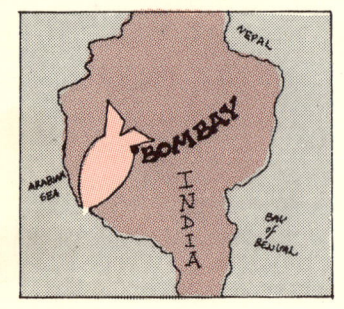

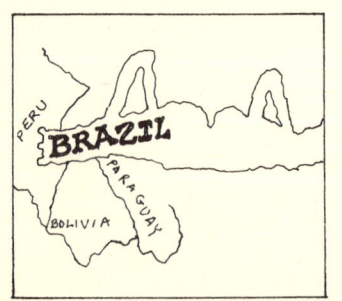

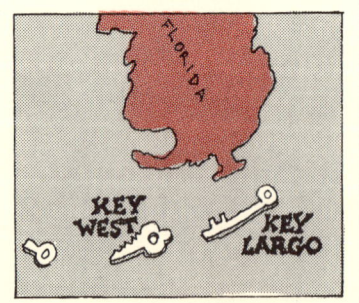

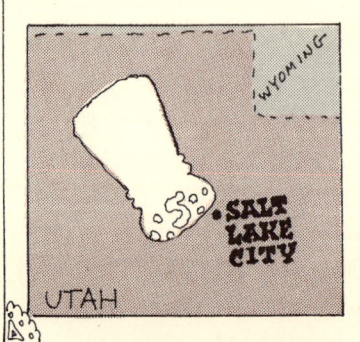

"I'd be lost without it!!"

HOTSTEIN WORLD ATLAST! BY LOB HOTSTEIN

Who put the pits in **Pittsburgh**?

What put the liver in **Liverpool**?

Whose hand made the **Finger Lakes**?

What's cookin' in **Chile**?

When <u>did</u> **DEATH** Valley die?

What KNOT to do in **Taiwan**!

ANT ARCTICA

BOMBAY, INDIA, NEPAL, ARABIAN SEA, BAY OF BENGAL

TURKEY, MEDITERRANEAN SEA, SYRIA

PERU, BRAZIL, PARAGUAY, BOLIVIA

FLORIDA, KEY WEST, KEY LARGO

UTAH, WYOMING, SALT LAKE CITY

LAKE ONTARIO, NEW YORK, FINGER LAKES, RYE

Pages and pages of full-color maps!
A textbook you can read upside down!

Just send $9.99 and a piece of your state in a jar to
ATLAST
3 Quotient Park
Continental Divide, North America

WHAT TO SAY WHEN THE TEACHER SAYS

Where's your homework?!!

Throw out those tired old excuses and say:

"It was stolen by an Egyptian historian who thought it was an example of early hieroglyphics."

"There was a power failure."

"The cat ate it."

"I sold it."

"My father took it to the office to show it off."

"My mother wallpapered the bathroom with it."

"I couldn't do it last night because my mother made me watch TV."

It's not FAIR when...

You've done all your homework all week and the teacher calls on you the one day you didn't do it!

page 76

SUPERTHINK introduces **I'VE GOT IT!** SUBJECT GUM

The only food for thought that you can chew... melts in your mind, not in your stomach!

Made from a blend of secret herbs discovered over a hundred years ago by a farmer in Foolinaround, Iowa. Until now, used only by his descendants... now available to you through the only distributor: Superthink Company, the manufacturer of I'VE GOT IT. Get yours today!

Comes in 4,028 delicious subject flavors:

- SUCCULENT spelling
- PEPPERMINT grammar
- Yum-Yum fractions
- APPLE PIE piano
- PICKLE penmanship
- cranberry american history
- base 5 ALIVE
- ALL Flavor digestive system

One bite and you're smart again! Eliminates the need for tutors! No more test worries! And if your mom asks about cavities, just show her the I'VE GOT IT seal:

You too can become a dentist; chew 25 packages of I'VE GOT IT in a week, and... you'll have it! Won't stick to braces or bite plates!

page 77

This glorious painting can be yours!
Each one signed by the artist!
Framed in unusual bus tire frames!
UNIQUE!
A collector's item!
Limited edition of only 7 billion!

ASSEMBLY Assembly Kit

page 78

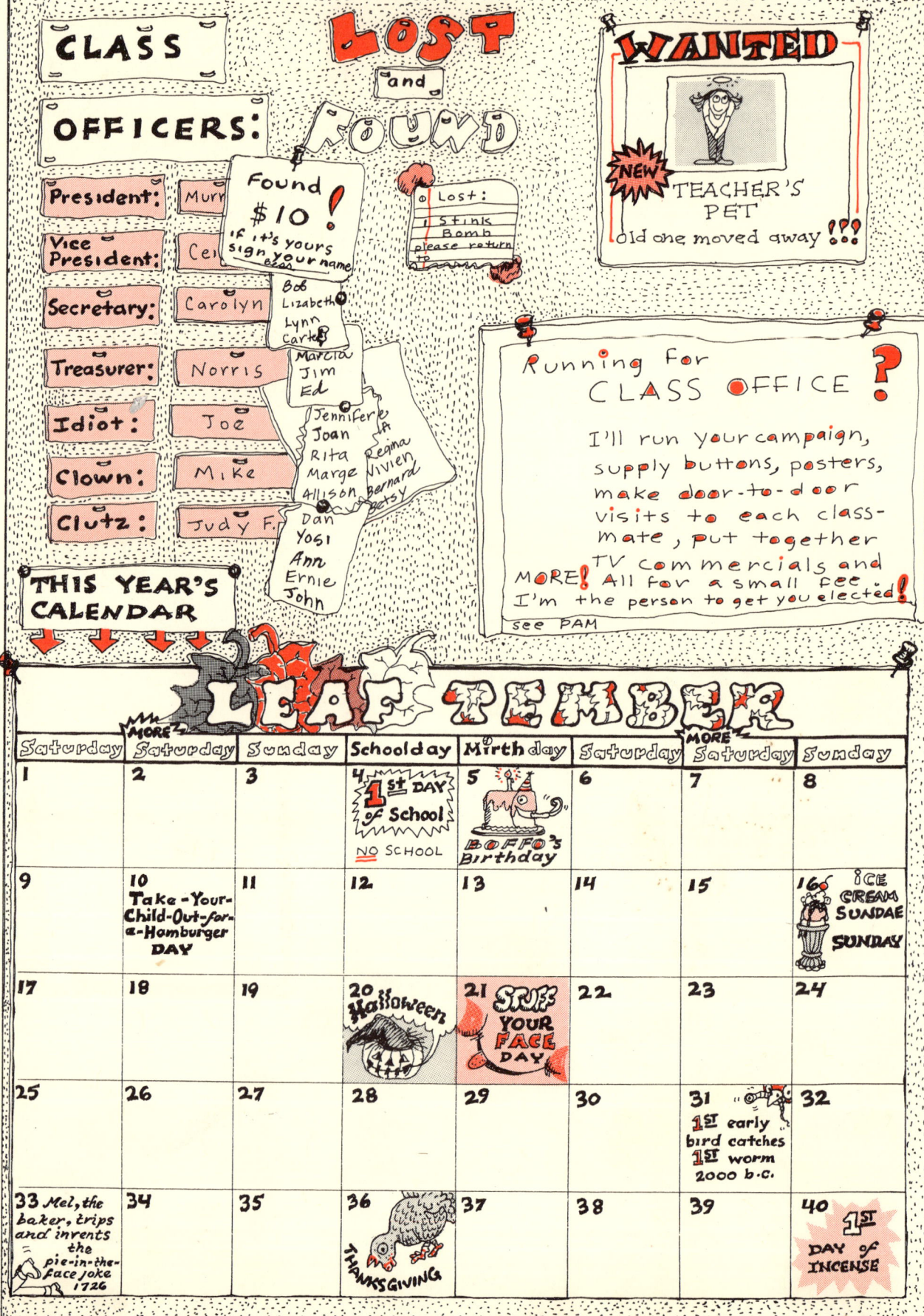

CLASS OFFICERS:

- **President:** Murr...
- **Vice President:** Ce...
- **Secretary:** Carolyn
- **Treasurer:** Norris
- **Idiot:** Joe
- **Clown:** Mike
- **Clutz:** Judy F.

LOST and FOUND

Found $10! If it's yours sign your name

Lost: 1 Stink Bomb please return to...

Bob, Lizabeth, Lynn, Carter, Marcia, Jim, Ed, Jennifer, Joan, Rita, Marge, Allison, Regina, Vivien, Bernard, Betsy, Dan, Yosi, Ann, Ernie, John

WANTED
NEW TEACHER'S PET — old one moved away!!!

Running for CLASS OFFICE?

I'll run your campaign, supply buttons, posters, make door-to-door visits to each classmate, put together TV commercials and MORE! All for a small fee. I'm the person to get you elected!
see PAM

THIS YEAR'S CALENDAR

LEAFTEMBER

Saturday	Saturday	Sunday	Schoolday	Mirthday	Saturday	MORE Saturday	Sunday
1	2	3	4 — 1st DAY of School — NO SCHOOL	5 — BOFFO's Birthday	6	7	8
9	10 — Take-Your-Child-Out-for-a-Hamburger DAY	11	12	13	14	15	16 — ICE CREAM SUNDAE SUNDAY
17	18	19	20 — Halloween	21 — STUFF YOUR FACE DAY	22	23	24
25	26	27	28	29	30	31 — 1st early bird catches 1st worm 2000 b.c.	32
33 — Mel, the baker, trips and invents the pie-in-the-face joke 1726	34	35	36 — THANKSGIVING	37	38	39	40 — 1st DAY of INCENSE

SNOWUARY

Saturday	MORE Saturday	Sunday	Schoolday	Mirthday	Saturday	MORE Saturday	Sunday
1	2	3	4	5 LEGAL SNOW DAY	6	7	8
9 NATIONAL Down Jacket DAY	10	11	12 Christmas Chanuka VACATION	13	14	15	16
17	18	19	20 Christmas Chanuka VACATION	21	22	23	24
25	26	27	28 NEW YEAR'S	29	30	31	32
33	34	35	36	37	38 Kid's DAY	39	40

RAINPRIL

1	2	3	4	5	6	7	8
CATCH-A-RUNNING-NOSE WEEK...							
9	10	11	12 Valentine's DAY School Closed	13	14	15	16
17	18 NATIONAL UN-BIRTHDAY DAY	19	20	21	22	23	24
25	26	27	28 APRIL FOOL'S DAY School Closed	29	30	31	32
33	34	35	36	37	38	39 SPRUNG SOLSTICE	40

BLOOMUNE

1	2	3	4 PET'S DAY	5	6	7	8
9	10	11	12 SLEEP LATE DAY	13	14	15	16
17	18	19	20	21 T-T-Shirt DAY	22	23	24
25 BLAST THE STEREO EVE	26	27	28	29	30	31 United Federation of Kids Founded 1978	32
33	34	35	36 LAST DAY of SCHOOL NO SCHOOL	37	38	39	40

SWIMULY-SNEAKERGUST

1	2	3	4 FOURTH WORKS	5	6	7	8
9	10 International Graffiti DAY	11	12 Summer Vacation	13	14	15	16
17	18	19	20	21	22	23	24 LAST DAY of FRISPO
25	26	27	28	29	30	31	32
33	34	35	36	37	38	39 PEELING DAY	40

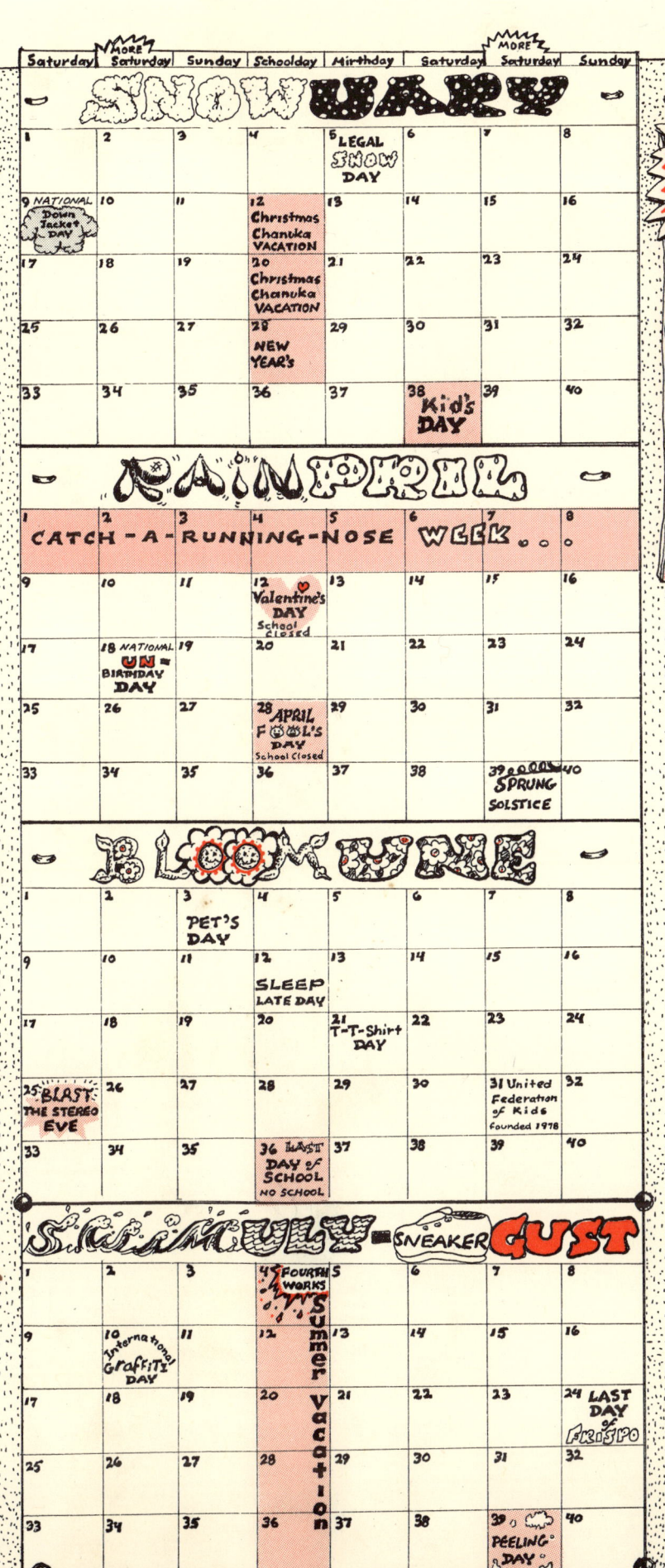

COMING ATTRACTIONS:

Coming Soon...
to your desk:
MATH TEST
☆ Starring ☆
the person who studies

REWARD

For information leading to the capture of the person who left a tack on my chair.

see Libby Sue

PLEASE Do **NOT** stick any more notes up with **BUBBLE GUM!**

page 79

THE OPEN MOUTH TUTORING SERVICE

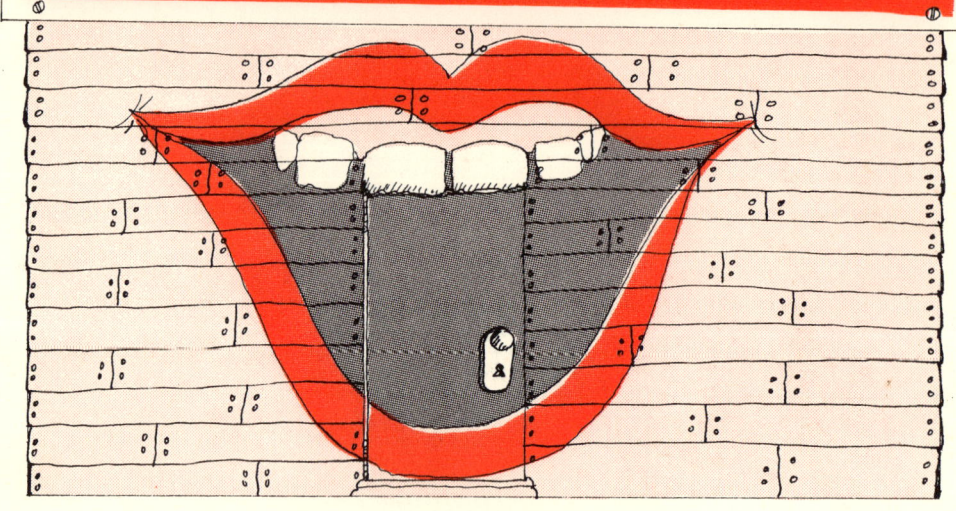

owned and operated by kids,
for kids . . . specializing in helping you do those hard things
that always look so easy!

Ear Wiggling

Finger Snapping

Gum Cracking and Pulling

Bubble Blowing

Burping on Command

Whistling

Advanced Whistling—
Two fingers in mouth

Winking

Long-distance
Water Fountain Spraying

Bite Plate Clicking

Magic Tricks

and new this year—
Playing Music
on a Blade of Grass
and Remedial Courses
in Lanyard Making!

Mirth's WRETCHED CLASS PICTURE AWARD

page 81

SCHANKEL'S SCHOOPONS

A unique subscription service—already 4,000 schools belong! Yearly fee: $4.59, and worth every penny (all four hundred and fifty-nine of them)!

When you're in a pickle, just whip out a SCHOOPON; it will save your day!!

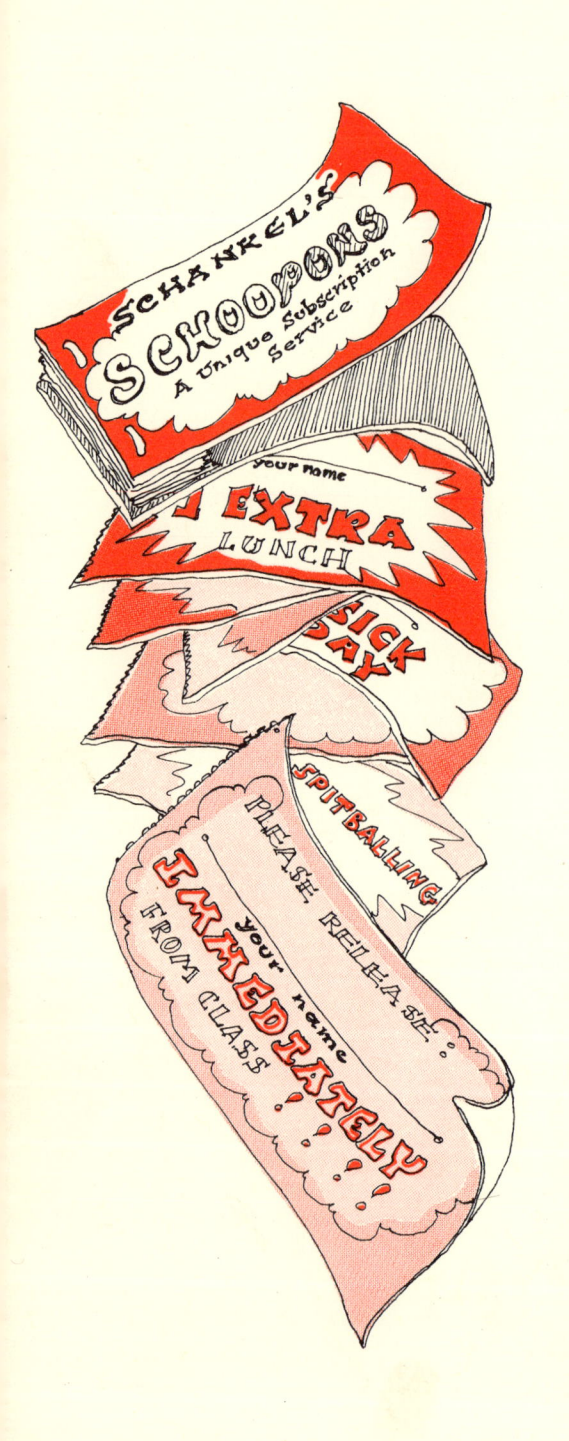

1 Extra lunch

1 Sick day

1 Free school day cut (no note from home)

1 Free lateness (no note from home)

Erase one bad mark each:

    for talking

    for spitballing

    for paper airplaning

1 Automatic release if kept after class

1 Excuse from any meeting

1 Excuse from gym

1 Excuse just because it's spring

    Be the principal for a day

Plus MORE! Plus MORE! Plus MORE! including bonus blank SCHOOPONS Plus MORE! Plus MORE! Plus MORE!

US

page 83

Clean up your plate!

THE MIRTH DICTIONARY of PARENTAL EXPRESSIONS or what they really mean:

I'll give you something to cry about . . .

Do you think money grows on trees?

In one ear and out the other . . .

Do they teach you those words in school?

I'll eat my hat!

Your eyes are bigger than your stomach . . .

Do you think I'm made of money?

I might as well talk to the wall . . .

Clean up your plate!

Keep this list to use should you have children of your own.

You've had it soft 'til now,
but you'll see when you get to be my age!

It's not FAIR when...

...you've just made a gigantic sandcastle and your sister kicks it over!

...people step on your feet!

...the dog eats your favorite snack!

...your friend does something wrong for thirty minutes, and you do it for thirty seconds and get caught!

...you have to go visit relatives when you planned to play in the snow!

...you get stuck with the hand-me-downs!

...your parents don't believe you!

JOIN United Federation of Kids TODAY!

Our Motto: 👫 R not 🐐🐐

UFK REPRESENTATIVE WILL HELP YOU BARGAIN FOR:

better bedtime . . . less dishwashing and drying . . . TV privileges . . . weaker punishments . . . tastier school lunches

BENEFITS:

summer vacation with pay . . . guaranteed minimum allowance . . . parents not allowed to play favorites . . . **UFK** court rules on all disagreements . . . limited hours for chores

With your membership you WILL receive:

Membership card
Union button
Picket sign kit
THREE helpful booklets:

"Let's not get left in the dust!"
PATSY MARCIANO, President UFK

- HOW NOT TO STRIKE OUT
- HOW TO MARCH
- WHAT TO DO IF YOUR PARENTS WON'T LET YOU JOIN the UFK

United Federation of Kids — Kids are not Goats

MEMBERSHIP CARD

SIGN UP NOW!!!
48% have already joined!
REMEMBER . . .
there is strength in numbers!

correspondo

LETTER-KITS

**Guaranteed authentically handwritten letters—
they look as if you wrote them yourself!
Just sign your name! SAVES TIME! SAVES WORK!
Order NOW!
Allow six weeks
for delivery.**

Sampler Kit contains: Letters from Camp, Thank-you Letters, Everyday Notes (" . . . just thinking of you . . . ")

Handmade Card Assortment contains: Birthday cards, Mother's & Father's Day cards, Valentines, Assorted Holiday cards.

Good News stationery pads and matching envelopes say: " . . . just had to write and tell you that I _____ "

Handmade linoleum block print Christmas cards

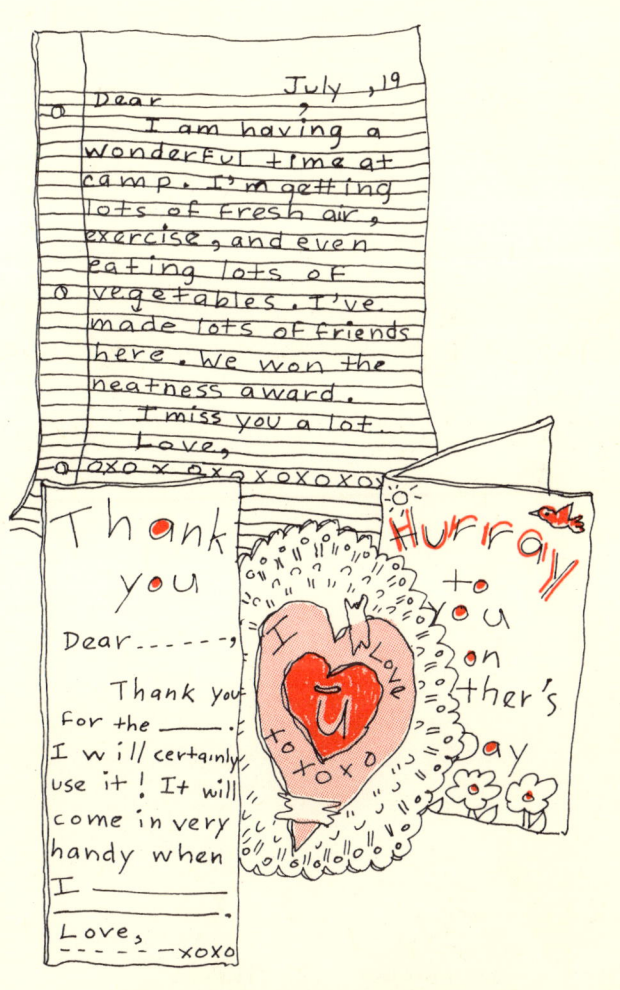

10 WAYS NOT TO CLEAN UP YOUR ROOM!

In the past you could:

Use a shovel

Hire three elves

Go on strike

Use mirrors

Sweep everything under the bed

Throw everything into . . . boxes, the closet, your brother's room, or heave it all out the window!

BUT NOW there's INSTANT All Purpose CLEAN ROOM

Just send $5.95 and all your dirty underwear along with a photo of your room all cleaned up.

NO SPRAYS!

NO MESSY CLEANSERS!

This will be the *last* time you ever have to straighten it!

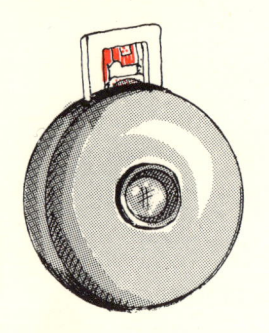

You will receive by 12th-class mail our handy easy-to-install peephole viewer and a full-color slide of your clean room. Insert slide into viewer. When your parent looks in, your room will always look as neat as the last day you cleaned it!!

We guarantee nothing — if not **entirely satisfied . . .** tough!

RECOGNIZING HOMOFAMILIUS

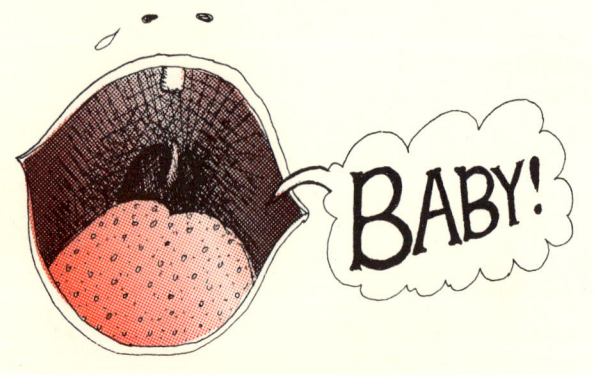

BABY!

has large mouth, snively nose, big ears, and leaves tracks and trails wherever it goes. Will sometimes team up with sleeping parent to get you in trouble. Plays with *your* things and misplaces them.

SLEEPING PARENT

mouth open, eyes shut, hand dangling off bed, couch, or chair. Hair is messy. Sometimes drooling. Makes loud snoring sounds like a horse. If awakened, can be very unpredictable, or get very angry, or even throw things! BEWARE!!

DOUBLE TROUBLE
incorporated

NOW you can be in 2 places at once!
Rent your own personal
look-alike double for
a day,
a minute,
an hour,
a week.
Visit our showroom
and see a complete stock of
YOUbots
100% BUBONIC with complex solid-state circuits

to cater to your every whim!

Feel like running away for a few days, but don't want
the hassles of worrying your parents or getting punished?

Rent a YOUbot. Just send your picture.
We will customize your bubonic wonder.
It delivers itself to you at no extra charge.

YOUbot is guaranteed to look, talk, and act just like you.
Simple manual explains how to program
YOUbot for whatever mission you assign it.

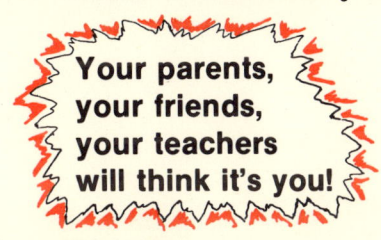

*Your parents,
your friends,
your teachers
will think it's you!*

INFINITE uses. 10 million available programs.
Moderate prices. Easy allowance downpayment plan.

Remember: YOU can play while YOUbot's in school.

page 90

Do you have a housebound pet???

Would it like a taste of WILD LIFE?

Today you can enroll your pet in

COMMUNIMAL

the intraplanetary communication network for pets.

We match indoor pets with animals in the wild. They exchange letters, photos, and tape cassettes telling each other about their different lives. Pets will find new meaning and joy as they expand their horizons.

COMMUNIMAL
REGISTRATION CARD

Please enroll _____
(pet's name)

in the intraplanetary communication network. I understand that it will be ideally matched with a correspondent living in the wild. Enclosed is 23¢ for my one-time only registration fee.

Your name _____

Address _____

_____

Pet's paw print

Paste
pet
photo
here

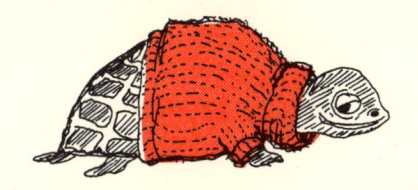

Turtle Neck

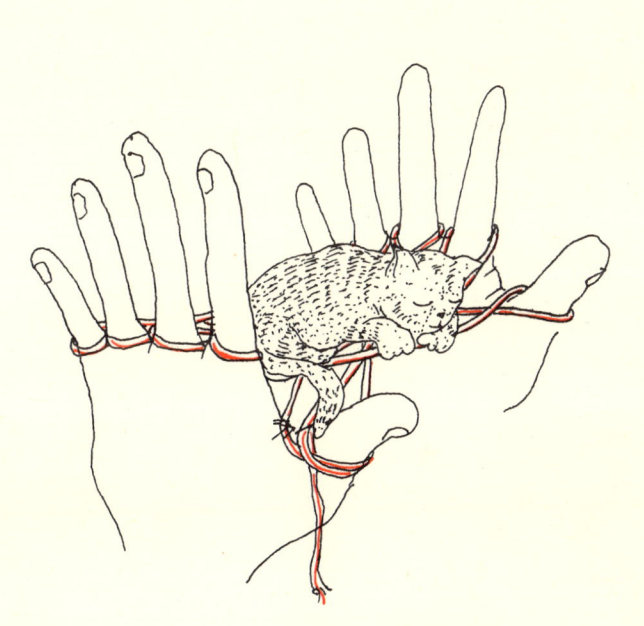

Cat's Cradle

Put your petal under your pillow . . .

Parents' Presents, INC.

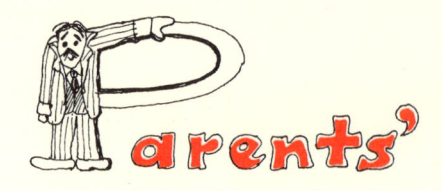

Presents bought by Parents for Parents

—No more worries . . .
—No more racking your brain . . .
—No more buying Dad ties . . .
—No more buying Mom hankies . . .

YOUR PARENTS' SATISFACTION GUARANTEED

Send now for a P.P. Information Questionnaire
Free surprise gift for all
those replying before midnight, December 2, 1922!

Before P.P.

After P.P.

BEWARE OF PLANT

11 WAYS TO DRIVE PARENTS CRAZY ON CAR TRIPS...

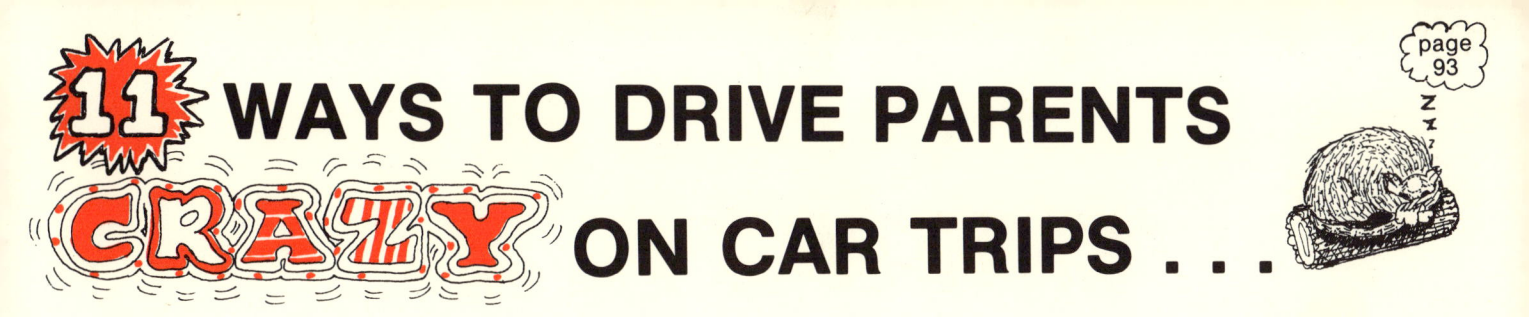

Ask to go to the bathroom just after the car has pulled out of the rest stop.

Roll your window up and down over and over while humming to yourself.

Ask every thirty-four seconds, "When are we going to get there???"

Call out license plate numbers, car makes, and road signs.

Fight with, tickle, tease, get hysterical with your brother, sister, friend, yourself.

Ask to sit in the front; play with the radio dials.

Ask to sit in the back; make nauseous sounds.

Sing this song:

> Nine million bottles of beer on the wall,
> Nine million bottles of beer,
> If one of those bottles should happen to fall...
> Eight million, nine hundred ninety-nine thousand, nine hundred ninety-nine bottles of beer on the wall!
> Eight million, nine hundred ninety-nine thousand, nine hundred ninety-nine bottles of beer on the wall,
> Eight million, nine hundred ninety-nine thousand, nine hundred ninety-nine bottles of beer,
> If one of those bottles should happen to fall...
> (and so on)

WHOOPEE INN

The perfect place to get away for a day, a weekend, a whole summer ...

Escape from the pressures of family life—no one over **16** allowed!

- Parent sitting service in comfortable cottages a day's ride away.
- Enjoy 20 different fast-food restaurants including: 24-hour soda fountain and sundae bar.
- Never required to use knife and fork; eat whatever you like!
- Visit the 101 room game arcade filled with every machine ever invented and each one is FREE! FREE! FREE!
- Every room is chock full of fun and surprises to delight and entertain you—wall size TV ... unlimited supply of pillows, comics ... quadraphonic stereo system ... marshmallow roaster ... free soda dispenser ... room service brings you anything! homework valet brings your homework to the door. Done!
- No Curfews—stay up as late as you want! sleep as late as you want!
- Swim indoors or out year round—6 pools including one with waves, salt, and surfboards.

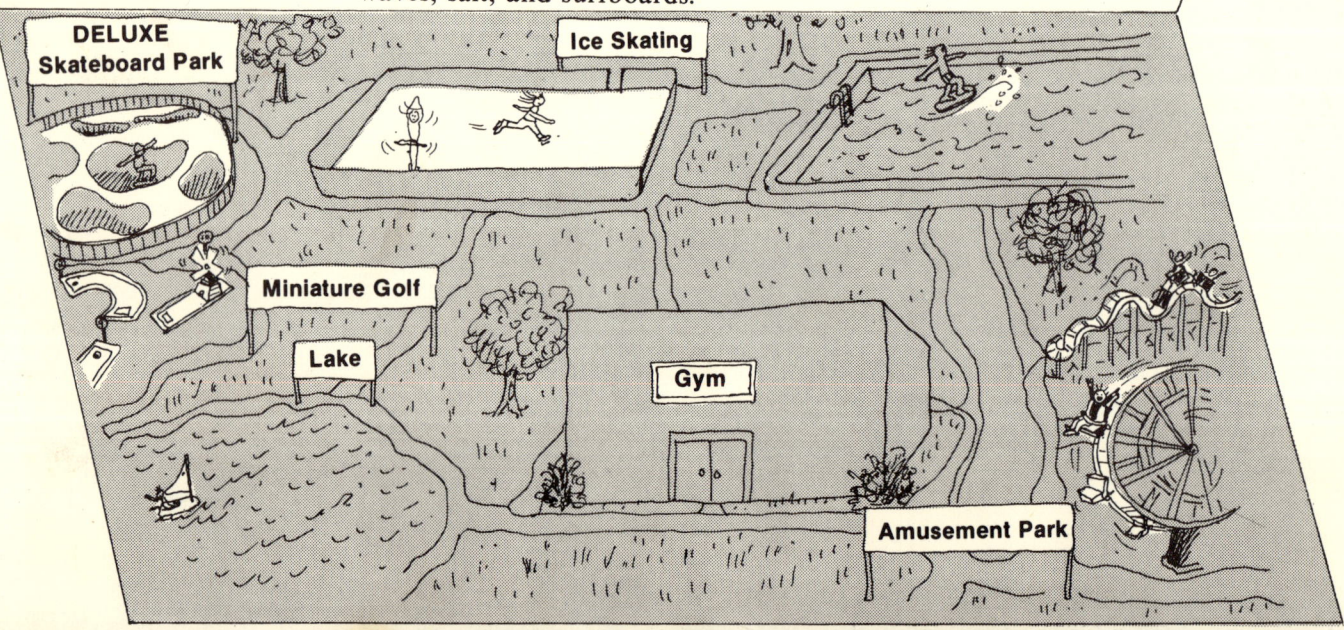

DELUXE Skateboard Park
Ice Skating
Miniature Golf
Lake
Gym
Amusement Park

How to Get Your Parents to Stop Smoking

Glue their cigarettes together.

Poke holes in their cigarettes.

Take the tobacco out.

Make small drawings of skulls and crossbones and paste them on
> cigarette packs,
> ashtrays,
> your parent's chest.

Cut out articles about how bad smoking is and mail them to your parents.

Cough and roll on the floor every time they light up.

Draw a picture of a dirty lung; give it to them as a Mother's/Father's Day card.

Make a doomsday construction by pasting their cigarettes together to look like a tombstone.

Make up a song, or a poem, or a play about why they should stop.

Get brochures from cancer and lung associations and leave them all over the house.

Hide matches and lighters.

Make up a list of 100 or 1,000 reasons why they should stop.

Give them a booklet of handmade coupons they can cash in for special rewards when they stop.

MOM AND POP PORTRAIT PILLOWS

Try this for real!

Ask your parents for some of their old clothes to make the body.

Use old sheets, decorative fabrics, or felt to make head, hands, feet, and features.

Use buttons, patches, zippers, and anything else you can sew or glue on for decorations.

Use yarn, string, or even a mop top for hair, eyebrows, and eyelashes.

You'll need: needles, pins, scissors, stuffing, and newspaper or paper bags.

Draw a life-size head on the paper and cut it out. Pin it on to the cloth you've chosen for the head. Double the cloth so you get two heads. Cut out the heads.

Put the two cloth circles together, outside facing in. Pin them together, and sew around the edge, leaving an opening about 4 inches (10.2 cm) long. Turn the cloth right-side out, and stuff. Stitch up the opening.

Cut out a pair of hands and feet. You could use the same method as you did for the head, or just use felt and leave the hands and feet flat.

Pin the head, hands, and feet onto the clothing. Sew on tight, but be sure to leave a large opening in the clothing to put stuffing into. Stuff the body until it's as full as you want it. Sew up your last opening.

Add hair, eyes, nose, mouth, a hat, a tie, whatever appeals to you. Make accessories such as a purse, or a briefcase, or a pipe to add to the pillow figure.

If you don't want the hassle of stuffing, just leave one big opening, and very firmly sew on a wide loop at the back of the head. Hang it up and PRESTO! a MOM or POP Laundry Bag! Do a portrait of yourself, too!